CHURCH AS SACRAMENT

Colm O'Doherty

Church as Sacrament

THE NEED FOR SELF-QUESTIONING

THE COLUMBA PRESS
DUBLIN 1994

First edition, 1994, published by
the columba press
93 The Rise, Mount Merrion, Blackrock, Co Dublin

ISBN 1 85607 062 X

Cover by Bill Bolger
Origination by The Columba Press
Printed in Ireland by
Genprint Ltd., Dublin

Contents

The Irish Churches in the Irish world may not take unto themselves the motto *Gaudium et Spes* until they first acknowledge their role in maintaining the *luctus et angor*, 'the grief and the anguish' of the people of our time (par.1).

— Enda Mc Donagh, 'A Church for the World'
in *Freedom to Hope?*
Edited by A Falconer, S MacRéamoinn, E McDonagh
The Columba Press, Dublin, 1985, p 91.

Introduction

Having been ordained in 1972 I lived and worked for most of my twenty years of priesthood – from which I resigned in 1992 – as a Roman Catholic curate in both town and country parishes in Northern Ireland. In that time thousands of people have been killed there and many thousands maimed as a result of the 'recent violence' which has been going on since August, 1968. Although it is almost a cliché to say that there is hardly a household in the North that has not been affected by the troubles; yet the truth of the statement, cliché or not, cannot be ignored.

Apart from the violence, Northern Ireland is also known – paradoxically, it might seem – for the high rate of church attendance among its population, both Catholic and Protestant. In my last parish, a country parish in County Derry, I would estimate that about 93% of Catholics attend church regularly. So it is to be expected that the troubles would figure in the course of pastoral work, quite explicitly as on occasions of death or injury to parishioners or others in the local community, and more generally in conversations and meetings with Catholics and Protestants in the area.

Let me here recall a few incidents, some minor and others more tragic, that have challenged me to consider how the church is meant to be in relation to the troubles; what do people expect of the Roman Catholic Church; can and should it meet these expectations; should it be trying to create other expectations?

Firstly a 'simple' incident in the parish: a young man (I will call him Michael) requests the use of the local church hall in which to hold practices for a republican band. Is there a simple 'yes' or 'no' to this request? A number of issues are to be considered and among them are:

1. A republican band exists in the parish, although at present practising outside the parish.
2. Michael considers it appropriate to approach the priest with this request.
3. What is a republican band; where does it march; when and with whom?
4. What is its relationship with any of the political, or non-political, republican movements?
5. What are the implications of a 'yes' in the context of the local community, which is about 50% Catholic and 50% Protestant?
6. What are the implications of a 'no' in relation to the twenty-five band members, members of the parish?

There are many implications for the community, the church and the priest, no matter what the decision might be regarding Michael's request.

A second incident: a republican funeral. Funerals and burial services of I.R.A. members, as well as being times of distress and grief among family and friends, have been occasions of bitter controversy between the I.R.A. and church authorities. The I.R.A. has been accused of manipulating families and funerals for its own propaganda purposes, while it, in turn, has accused church authorities, at times, of trying to deny the right of a Christian service and burial to one of its number.

I have never received from church authorities any instructions on how such services might be conducted. I presume that one should bury I.R.A. members in the same way that one conducts any other funeral service. But among the issues that have to be considered are:

1. Even before the funeral, at the wake, what is the attitude and practice of the priest when there are uniformed I.R.A. colleagues of the deceased standing guard at the head of the coffin?

2. Is the priest to walk in front of a funeral procession when the coffin is draped with the tricolour, with possibly mask, gloves and dark glasses (all worn by active I.R.A. members) placed on the tricolour?

3. Is the draped coffin permitted to enter church grounds or the church itself?

4. In the funeral homily what, if anything, might the priest say of the deceased and of the circumstances of his or her death?

5. At the graveside, what about orations or shootings over the coffin; what is the priest to do if agreements he had made beforehand with those responsible for the funeral are not adhered to?

6. How to respond to media requests for comment or statement?

To some these may seem minor liturgical or ritual questions, but people will interpret one's behaviour in such situations as being indicative of a personal and institutional attitude towards violence. So whether the priest likes it or not, he carries responsibility for expressing the church's attitude in how he responds to such questions as posed above.

And thirdly, statements from the hierarchy. Many of these have been made public through the national press, but on one occasion – apart from the Pastoral of 1975, *Human Life is Sacred*[1] – all the priests of Ireland were asked by the bishops to read a statement at all masses: the statement of November 9, 1987, issued in the name of the Irish Episcopal Conference, following the Enniskillen bombing and the kidnapping in Dublin of Mr John O'Grady After naming the two events the statement goes on to say :

Point 5. There is no room for ambivalence. In face of the present campaign of republican violence the choice of all Catholics is clear. It is a choice between good and evil.

Point 6. It is sinful to join organisations committed to violence or to remain in them. It is sinful to support such organisations or to call on others to support them. [2]

While these and other points are congruent with the many statements the church has made about violence, there remains a number of pastoral questions to be answered, for instance:

11

1. The priests were told that the statement was 'to be read at all masses.' Was the priest to make any form of comment on the statement?
2. How was it to be pastorally applied? For instance, if known Sinn Fein members came to communion, what should the priest do?
3. What is the meaning in the statement of 'sinful'? Is it the same as 'wrong'?
4. Is it as simple as: 'it is a choice between good and evil'? What about 'the good people' who support republican movements?

These questions raise the issue of the church being primarily known for its statements of condemnation. Whenever the priest speaks in the Sunday homily about violent incidents in the locality, there is the trap of thinking that moral leadership can be given through condemnation alone. It remains a challenge, while not avoiding condemnation, always to speak in a way that encourages people to live out of the positive vision of hope proclaimed by the resurrection, and to trust in the compassion of the God who knows the inner disposition of each individual, the God who 'created my inmost being, and knit me together in my mother's womb.'(Ps 139:13) This book is the outcome of reflection and conversation on how to meet this pastoral challenge.

It seems to me that such a challenge requires us to examine the broader issue of the nature of church, to ask what the church is. Then in the light of that, I consider critically how the Roman Catholic Church is, and might newly be, in a particular situation at a particular time – in Northern Ireland during the present troubles. And although I focus on the Roman Catholic Church I think there are implications for other churches. There is at present a 'serious desire in many churches for an ecumenical study on ecclesiology.'[3] In recent years ecclesiology has become one of the principal areas of interest and importance in ecumenical debate. We are in a 'theological high season in ecclesiology.'[4]

Although it is not absolutely clear what kind of ecclesiology the churches are demanding, it is acknowledged that 'during the last fifteen years a reception of the idea of the church as sacrament has taken place in ecumenical debate.'[5] With an eye to such acceptance, but primarily because of the centrality of this theme in Roman Catholic thinking, as evidenced in the documents of Vatican II[6] I have chosen this theological concept of the church as sacrament as the means of examining the nature of the church.

In preparing this book I have been greatly helped by Bishop Edward Daly, recently resigned as Bishop of Derry, and by Cardinal Cahal Daly – when he was Bishop of Down and Connor. Both men gave me access to many of their homilies and talks over the years. While I acknowlede the importance of their contribution, the gospel offers a challenge to the Northern situation which invites on-going reflection.

In chapter 1 the theology of the church as sacrament is examined under three headings: *christological*, as that is the context within which ecclesiology is now so often studied; *pastoral*, that being the setting in which people experience church; and *eschatological*, because ultimately the church is for the kingdom, and can be understood only in such terms.

In chapter 2 statements from the Roman Catholic hierarchy are considered and then examined as to how they reflect the theology of chapter 1, under the same three headings as above.

In chapter 3 an understanding of the church as sacrament is presented that is in tune with the theological thrust of chapter 1, but according to different categories of thought, namely *suspicion* and *otherness*, themes that can take into account the context of Northern Ireland.

In chapter 4 the bishops' response to the violence is found to be wanting in the light of this new understanding, and I conclude with some concrete suggestions as to how this understanding could alter their response.

Notes

1. Irish Catholic Bishops, *Justice, Love and Peace: Pastoral Letters of the Irish Bishops 1969-1979*, Dublin, Veritas, 1979.
2. Statement from Irish Episcopal Conference, issued by the Standing Committee of the Irish Bishops on 9 November, 1987.
3. Houtepen, Anton: 'Towards an Ecumenical Vision of Church.' *One in Christ* Vol 3, 1989, pp 217-237, p 220. As evidence of this desire Houtepen goes on to list references from the six volumes, Thurian, Max (ed.) *Churches Respond to B E M*, Faith and Order Paper No.111, W.C.C., Geneva, p 220.
4. Houtepen, op cit supra (n 3), p 218.
5. Gassmann, Gunther 'The Church as Sacrament, Sign and Instrument' in Limouris, Gennadios (ed.) *Church, Kingdom, World*, Faith and Order Paper No 130, Geneva, W.C.C., 1986, pp 1-17, p 1.
6. Abbott, Walter (gen.ed.) *The Documents of Vatican II*, New York, Guild Press, 1966, *Lumen Gentium*, p 15, par 1; p 79, par 48.
   See also *Gaudium et Spes*, p 247, par 45; *Sacrosanctum Concilium*, p 140, par 5.

CHAPTER 1

Church as Sacrament

1. CONTEXT

If 'The People of God' was the most popular notion of church after Vatican II, it was not necessarily the most important. According to Schmaus:

> the total sacramentality of the Church is probably the most important pronouncement it (Vatican II) made concerning the Church... All the Council's other statements about the Church are affected by this one. [1]

It would seem that it was the deliberate intention of the bishops in the Council for it to be this way, because sacrament is the very first concept named regarding the church in what is accepted as the foundation document of Vatican II, *Lumen Gentium*:

> By her relationship with Christ, the Church is a kind of sacrament or sign of intimate union with God and of the unity of all mankind. She is also an instrument for the achievement of such union and unity.[2]

It is obvious from the textual history of the document that the decision by the Council to use such language was quite deliberate. The initial draft of the document said nothing about the sacramental nature of the church, and there was much criticism about the spirit and approach of the text. It was said to have been triumphal, clerical and legal in tone, and not enough attention was given to the pastoral dimension. In the light of these criticisms a second draft was proposed and it is in this text that the notion of sacrament appears. It is clear that in this case it was recommended as a term to help counteract the triumphalist tone of the first draft. (Nevertheless, we shall see later that it is on the very grounds of it being triumphalist that some churches object to the term.) In spite of opposition from some of the bishops to the term, it not being biblical, there was a general welcome for it and it was to appear in some later paragraphs as well as in other Council documents, e.g. *Sacrosanctum Concilium*.[3]

Despite the non-biblical source of the term, a sacramental view of the church is to be found among the Fathers from Cyprian through Ambrose and Augustine.[4] The theme was recovered in the last century, and developed more fully in the present century by such authors as Henri de Lubac,[5] Otto Semmelroth,[6] Karl Rahner,[7] and Edward Schillebeeckx.[8] By the time, then, of Vatican II the notion of the church as sacrament was certainly current in European theological circles and available to the bishops to inform their thinking about the nature of the church.

Equally so it is acknowledged in ecumenical writings that there is a common heritage of understanding regarding the church: 'The Church as a sacramental reality... is itself an article of apostolic faith.' [9] And the Church of England is on record as saying:

> Only an explicit common understanding of the nature of the Church and its role as a credible and effective sign, instrument and sacrament of salvation will provide a secure foundation for the reconciliation of Churches.[10]

2. THEOLOGICAL UNDERSTANDING

But what is the theological understanding of the concept of the church as sacrament? It is important to acknowledge that there is a whole series of images and concepts to describe the church, e.g. bride of Christ, body of Christ, people of God, and they are all needed to throw light on its richness.[11] Yet the concept of the church as sacrament is chosen because there is much therein that can challenge any particular church's self-understanding, pastorally and theologically. When we call the church a sacrament what do we understand by sacrament in this context? I will now consider the meaning of sacrament under three headings, sacrament as christological, pastoral and eschatological, and examine the implications of such a perspective for the church. While I will focus on the Roman Catholic Church these terms could validly apply also to a consideration of the Protestant Churches. But first a few words briefly explaining the reasons for choosing these three headings.

The church does not exist of itself nor for itself. It is situated within a christological context, and is seen to share in Christ's role of being mediator between God and humankind. The church is spoken of as the 'Bride of Christ' and the 'Body of Christ', the latter being:

> undoubtedly the most important of the images applied to the Church in the New Testament. It clearly proclaims the closest possible identification of the Church with Jesus Christ...[12]

Secondly, although what I am examining has implications for the church in general, I intend to approach the study by recognising the importance of the local situation and the idea of ecclesiology being constructed contextually.[13] I do so by situating the church in a particular geographical location and considering a specific pastoral problem, that of violence at present in Northern Ireland. Moreover, because people experience the church primarily in pastoral situations it is appropriate to consider the church as sacrament from the pastoral perspective. And it has already been noted above that in objecting to the first draft of *Lumen Gentium* the bishops at Vatican II demanded that more attention be paid to the pastoral profile of the church. Thirdly the eschatological dimension: the church is for the kingdom, a force on earth working towards the bringing about of the kingdom.

> ... both nature and mission of the church have an essentially eschatological dimension to them. Like all the sacraments (in the strict sense), the church in itself has a future reference to eternal glory...[14]

I am choosing not to start from a particular definition[15] of the church as sacrament. I think it more fruitful to look at the matter from these three angles and so discover what are the characteristics such a description of the church is highlighting.

(a) Christological

> The key to the new understanding of the Church (as sacrament) reached by the Council (Vatican II) is the teaching on the christocentric character of the church.[16]

By using the word sacrament (or sign, or instrument) in relation to the church it is being said that the church is not an autonomous or self-sufficient entity. It points beyond itself, immediately to Christ. It is clear that Vatican II is working from such an understanding. Every reference to the church as sacrament in *Lumen Gentium* is made in an explicit christological context.[17] It is 'in Christ' that the church is sacrament; hence it is Christ, not the church, which is the primal sacrament. It is this understanding that enabled the bishops at Vatican II to choose this term 'sacrament' in their effort to avoid the triumphalist identification of Christ with the church, which had been presented in an earlier draft of *Lumen Gentium*.[18]

The notion of Christ as sacrament can be traced back to the Fathers[19] and has been taken up by recent theologians such as Rahner[20] and Schillebeeckx.[21] It is in Christ that we know and connect with the love, mercy and salvation of God. 'At various times in the past and in various different ways,'(Heb 1:1) God is revealed to humankind, quite particularily through the history of Israel. This presence of God came to a climax when the Son was sent into the world in the person of Jesus Christ at the Incarnation. 'Christ is the historically real and actual presence of the eschatalogically victorious mercy of God.' [22]

The presence of Christ with us does not merely offer us a possibility of salvation, but rather in principle betokens that we are already accepted for salvation in Christ. What this means is that, again in principle, salvation cannot be arrested or cancelled. Not that everyone necessarily will be saved as each person still can choose between salvation and damnation. But that is not to say that 'history as a whole is still at the decision of mankind, with God awaiting the decision.'[23]

In Christ God has decided for the world's salvation. In Christ we have a visible, historical presence of God being reconciled to the world, of God's indwelling in the world. Hence Christ is the sacrament of God, at one and the same time being 'indicatory and revelatory'[24] of God, to and for humankind.

But if Christ is the sacrament, how can we then call the church sacrament? Surely this is claiming too much? Does this not give good grounds for the church to be accused of being triumphalist?[25] Is it not safer to call the church instrument or sign, and reserve the term sacrament for Christ himself, as many of the Protestant Churches seem to favour? Is there not at least the possibility of ambiguity – doctrinally and pastorally – in applying a term to the church that has primary reference to Christ, and hence a danger of divinising the church by seeming to equate it with Christ? There have been times when people have interpreted the church as being the Body of Christ, as if the church were 'Christ living on,' or 'the prolongation of the incarnation'. Such thinking has the Logos assume not only the individual nature of Christ, but also the whole of human nature, and hence extends the hypostatic union to include the church. Such an interpretation is ruled out by church teaching.[26] In ecclesiology the art is to avoid both the identification of Christ with the church (the Roman Catholic temptation) and the separation of Christ from the church, (the Protestant temptation) while at the same time not rejecting the distinction between Christ and the church. As has been indicated above, Vatican II chose the term sacrament to achieve this.

So how is the church the sacrament of Christ? It is in his life, death and resurrection that Christ reveals to us the saving love of God, and is rightly named the sacrament of God, 'the one and only saving primordial sacrament.'[27] Following the Ascension that presence of Christ is no longer visible to us. But Christ, through his Spirit, makes available to us the saving presence of his glorified humanity in the form of the church. Here the church is reflecting its awareness of the invisible element, the presence of the Spirit of Christ, which informs the visible church. Without the Spirit of Christ the church becomes 'an eternal welfare institute.'[28]

> Rising from the dead, he (Christ) sent his life-giving Spirit upon his disciples and through this Spirit has established his body, the Church, as the universal sacrament of salvation.[29]

The focus on the Spirit opens up the possibility of considering the church from a trinitarian perspective, which is an approach found in the work of Moltmann[30] and Boff.[31] But the traditional view of the church stressing the indwelling of the Holy Spirit focusses on the church as 'enriched with heavenly things'.[32] It is 'the Jerusalem which is above,'[33] 'the spotless spouse,'[34] 'the edifice of God,'[35] and as such, regards itself while on earth 'as an exile.'[36] Thus it is first and foremost something instituted from on high,'[37] the church as God meant it to be.

But the church as humankind experiences it is the historical church, the external reality, 'the earthly church,'[38] that lives in the midst of 'trial and tribulation'[39] and is marked by 'afflictions and hardships which assail her from within and without,'[40] the church 'not without shadows.'[41] These are not two separate churches nor two separate realities, but rather the church looked at from two points of view, the former with the focus on the divine institution, and the latter focusing on the church 'insofar as she is an institution of men *and women* here on earth'[42] (italics, my addition).

Even though *Lumen Gentium* is very explicit when it says: 'they (the earthly church and the church enriched with heavenly things) form one interlocked reality which is comprised of a divine and a human element,'[43] there is evidence that the Council at times emphasised inappropriately the church's divine aspect, and hence as almost out of place in the world, a church 'journeying in a foreign land.'[44] The most explicit expression of this viewpoint occurs in the Council's document on ecumenism.[45] In order to avoid having the document read: 'During its pilgrimage on earth, this People, though still liable to sin,' the Pope, with the Council's agreement, amended the text to read: 'During its pilgrimage on earth, this People, though in its members liable to sin.'[46] We read in a footnote: 'Pope Paul added 'in its members' and thus the sentence avoids saying that the church is liable to sin.'[47]

It would appear that there is some reluctance to see the church as existing in the tension created out of its historical and its eternal nature, its human and divine elements. Where this tension is not maintained, the church inevitably overclaims for itself and runs the risk of being seen to equate itself with the presence of Christ on earth, and so fall prey to the triumphalism that Vatican II tried to avoid. This can lead to a defensive disposition on the part of the church to any critical comment, and can make it very difficult, even for the committed, to invite the church to engage in self-criticism. We need to understand such statements as: 'The church is the visible realisation of the saving reality of Christ in history,' [48] as much a challenge as a claim. It is not just a description of the church but, as a statement of potentiality, it is a reminder of its task. Rahner points to such a christologically-oriented church when he says:

> The church exists in the full sense, in the highest degree of actual fulfillment of her nature, by teaching, bearing witness to Christ's truth, bearing the cross of Christ through the ages, loving God in her members...[49]

(b) Pastoral

The above quotation tells us that the church is truly christological in its being fully pastoral. It is inevitable that there is a strong overlapping between these two dimensions. This mission of Christ, on which sacrament is based, shapes the nature of the church's pastoral presence. Vatican II says:

> This mission (of the Church) is a continuing one. In the course of history it unfolds the mission of Christ himself,

who was sent to preach the gospel to the poor. Hence, prompted by the Holy Spirit, the Church must walk the same road which Christ walked.'[50]

The mission and ministry of Christ, participating in the *missio Dei*, is frequently described in terms of Christ being Priest, Prophet and King.[51] These terms highlight the eschatological aspect of his ministry and can be complemented by other terms which point to Christ's mission to the world, e.g. by concentrating on his work of liberating and healing. The pastoral work of healing was very central to his mission and therefore he became familiar with what is weak and broken in human nature. To be the sacrament of Christ is to be marked with the same pastoral zeal and care as Jesus had, and hence to be present to the world in its brokenness. As sacrament the church must participate in both the transcendent and the immanent world, enabling and embodying the breakthrough of the former into the brokenness of the latter. There is a danger that the balance of these two elements is not always maintained, and hence the tension that is creative of sacrament disappears.

Just as Jesus came for the world, the church is for the world, remains alive by being connected with the world, and cannot define itself independent of the world. But how is the church to be for the world, how is it to fulfil such a calling? The pastoral response of the church has taken many forms. But a church that has an inclination to lay undue emphasis on its divine origins can hardly avoid the temptation to stand at some distance from the world and order it about, or else engage with the world with the purpose of conquering it. Both of these modes of relating to the world are ignoring, and are contrary to, the way of Jesus who 'was made flesh and came to dwell among us,' (Jn 1:14) and again who 'did not cling to his equality with God but emptied himself to assume the condition of a slave...' (Phil 2:6,7)

In entering into our nature, Jesus identified fully with our brokenness, and this remains the task and challenge for the church. Jesus wept with the bereaved, fed the hungry, struggled with temptation and experienced abandonment by God and humankind. One of the marks, therefore, of the pastoral dimension of the church as sacrament is that of being a servant church, a suffering church. This calls the church to know of brokenness not just of another or from the outside, but above all from within itself, from its own incompleteness and poverty.

The church itself, in calling the world to its proper end, must acknowledge its own historical nature and character as also being on the way, incomplete. While this perspective was not absent from the deliberations of the bishops at Vatican II who spoke of the church's 'need of being purified,'[52] we again see them making distinctions: it is not the church which fails but rather 'the members fail to live by them (all the means of grace) with all the fervour they should.'[53]

Could it be that in the Roman Catholic Church there is a holding back from fully acknowledging the fact that the church itself, being a social institution, participates in the faults and failings of any institution? Even more seriously, does this reflect a tendency in the Roman Catholic Church to deny its own human dimension and thereby inevitably weaken its pastoral potential? If so, it is thereby wanting to deny the humanity of God, expressed in Christ, and as a result is becoming idolatrous by wanting to be more 'divine' than God is. There is no doubt that this would affect the pastoral practice of the church, and also its pastoral credibility. 'A church that cannot tell or admit the truth about itself cannot be an authentic instrument for uncovering the truth of and about God.'[54] Could it be that the Roman Catholic Church can, at times, 'ab-use' the divine institution of the church as an escape clause to avoid its own brokenness and 'shadowed way',[55] and thereby weaken its pastoral potential?

(c) Eschatological
There would seem to be fairly general agreement among the churches in viewing the church in an explicitly eschatological con-

text.[56] This follows the main thrust of the life of Jesus whose message was the good news of the coming kingdom. Jesus, in word and deed, not only proclaimed the kingdom as coming, but witnessed to it as present: 'If I, by the finger of God, cast out devils, the kingdom of God has come upon you.' (Lk 11:20) It is the call and challenge of the church 'to complete his work on earth.'[57] But this is no easy task, especially because of the 'already-not yet' dialectic nature of the kingdom. On the one hand there is a tendency to interpret the kingdom in quite secularist terms, consciously or unconsciously identifying it with some earthly goal. This approach would see the good of the kingdom as being entrusted to humankind who would carry full responsibility for its achievement. On the other hand the kingdom could be taken to mean a reality which is totally otherworldly, without any significance or relevance attaching to the realities of this world. But neither approach does justice to the kingdom nor to humankind:

> We are otherworldly, or we are secular – but in either case this means we no longer believe in God's kingdom. Wanderers who love the earth aright do so only because it is on this earth that they make their approach to that alien land which they love above all else, except for which they would not be wandering at all. Only wanderers of this kind, who love both earth and God at the same time, can believe in the Kingdom of God.'[58]

Those seeking and living the kingdom are wanderers or pilgrims, and the church is a pilgrim people still on its way to completion. It has not always been easy for the church to sustain such a self-perception and the temptation has been, and most likely will continue to be, for the church to claim the kingdom for itself, and even to present itself as the realised kingdom over against the world, and hence avoid the eschatological tension and challenge.

Like Christianity itself, 'as life between passover and parousia,'[59] the church must always strain towards the completion signalled by: 'Maranatha, Come Lord Jesus', (Rev 22:20) while at the same time be always in the presence of that same Lord Jesus. It is the very nature of sacrament to exist in this same tension, at one and the same time to point towards and also make present. While being part of the immanent world the sacrament invites the eschatological to break through:

> A sacrament is something eschatological in the sense that the 'eschaton', the heavenly salvation we have yet to reach, has already invaded this world in the sacramental sign and is caught in an earthly element as in a seal.'[60]

Despite what may now seem to be a most obvious characteristic of the church, it was not without a struggle that the bishops at Vatican II accepted such a perspective. Yet in the end the bishops entitled chapter 7 of *Lumen Gentium*, 'The Eschatological Nature of the Pilgrim Church, and her Union with the Heavenly Church'. In that chapter they say: 'the church will attain her full perfection only in the glory of heaven.'[61] This is a statement of great importance. The church itself, by its nature and calling, is provisional, to be taken up in time to be renewed in Christ – the process of ecclesiogenesis.[62] The church is be-coming; it 'is always on the proclamation of her own provisional status and of her historically advancing elimination in the coming Kingdom of God towards which she is expectantly travelling.'[63] The church does not belong ultimately to itself but is a servant church, serving the kingdom, being of service to those seeking the kingdom and living values that witness to the kingdom.

Being eschatological in nature, the church is challenged to be open to on-going renewal in every sphere of its existence and to avoid any expression of sclerotic self-sufficiency. As it points the way towards completion, and hence informed by a 'spirit of caution and reserve about the present accomplishments of man *and woman* and the contemporary realisation of the kingdom of God, she must be prepared to criticise, to expose difficiencies, to exhort to repentance, and so forth'[64] (italics, my addition). It is incumbent on the church to hear the message it preaches to others and to be open to the same challenges and cautions. 'Judgement must begin at the house of God.' (1 Pet 4:17)[65]

Furthermore, while dealing with the eschatological nature of the church, Vatican II talks of the church as 'the universal sacrament of salvation',[66] recalling what it said earlier in the same document, when it called the church, 'the instrument of the redemption of all.'[67] The church is not a closed system, existing for the good and welfare of its members. It can be the universal sacrament of salvation only by being open to the world for the sake of the kingdom. It is not for the church to conquer the world, as such a perspective springs from an ecclesiology of combat rather than of saving. The church is to be in the world in service, witness and proclamation. In a spirit of co-operation and challenge the church, as sacrament for the world, invites us to engage fully with the world out of a kingdom vision of healing and renewal.'The church is frequently viewed as an agent for the transformation of the world according to the pattern of the Kingdom of God.'[68] And its calling is universal, which does not necessarily mean that everyone in the world is destined to become a member of the church. But it does inform the church as to its disposition: open and ready to embrace all peoples. Can the church, therefore, choose to whom it will address itself? What about a church that chooses one group over another; can it still claim to be true to its calling as the sacrament of the kingdom of God? I will come back to this question in chapters 3 and 4.

In summary, while it is acknowledged that 'there is no definition of sacrament in the constitution (*Lumen Gentium*) and no explanation of how the term is exactly to be applied to the church,'[69] nevertheless we have seen that its use has been most deliberate. This is why it is so important to have given serious consideration to whatever might help us understand the meaning of the church as sacrament. In so naming it we highlight that the church is pointing beyond itself, it is not for itself, and in a way it is not even itself. The church's full identity is forever outside and beyond itself. Because of its relation to Christ in his 'being' and the kingdom in its 'coming', it can only be by be-coming.

And so as sacrament it points in two directions: to the immanent and to the transcendent. The church is where both these elements can mutually indwell and dialogue with each other. The church, therefore, will always dwell in a dialectic tension and it is of its very nature to do so. It is to live constantly in the dialogue between its divine institution and its human embodiment, not alternating between these poles but incorporating both at the same time. It will continue to draw people towards itself but always guide them past itself to the fundamental sacrament, Christ, embodying the love of God. As sacrament it is to enter into situations, and know from the inside, of human brokenness and pain, and yet proclaim hope, and effect wholeness and unity. It will continue to move towards its own eschatological fulfillment while all the time remaining alive to its 'shadowed way.'[70] It is a church therefore in the process of be-coming, and sees itself as both gift and task, a presence of Christ given and yet to be realised. It is open to give to and receive from the world, to proclaim the kingdom and receive such proclamation itself. While present to the brokenness of the world and to its own brokenness, its message is one of hope and of a richer future for all peoples.

The view of the church that has emerged out of understanding it as sacrament is not the sole possession of any one denomination. It relates to each of the churches recovering a view of the church that has been long in the tradition but has not been to the fore in recent centuries. Because of the different histories of the denominations, they carry to sacramental ecclesiology different emphases. And while this examination of the church as sacrament draws on the Roman Catholic tradition, there is nothing therein contrary to the wisdom of the other denominations. Rather the different views enrich and fill out each other, whether it be the description of the church as sacrament in the Roman Catholic tradition, which underlines Christ's presence already in the church; or the W.C.C. tradition[71] which emphasises the Christ presence entering the world. This latter tradition offers a conviction about the earthed and sinful nature of the church to the Roman tradition which can be tempted to view church more from the transcendent perspective.

Notes
1. Schmaus, Michael: *The Church as Sacrament*, London, Sheed and Ward, 1975, p 5.
2. Abbott, Walter (gen. ed.) :*The Documents of Vatican II*, New York, Guild Press, 1966, *Lumen Gentium*, p 15, par 1.
3. Abbott: op cit supra (n 2), *Sacrosanctum Concilium*, p 140, par 5; *Gaudium et Spes*, p 247, par 45.
4. Kress, Robert: *The Church: Communion, Sacrament, Communication*, New York, The American Press, 1966, pp 118-126.
5. de Ludac, Henri: *Catholicism*, A Study of Dogma in Relation to the Corporate Destiny of Mankind, London, Burns and Oates, 1950.
6. Semmelroth, Otto: *Church and Sacrament*, Indiana, Fides, 1965.
7. Rahner, Karl: *The Church and the Sacraments*, London, Burns and Oates, 1963.
8. Schillebeeckx, Edward: *Christ the Sacrament*, London, Sheed and Ward, 1963.
9. Houtepen, Anton: 'Towards an Ecumenical Vision of Church.' *One in Christ* Vol 3, 1989, pp 217-237, p 227.
10. Thurian, Max (ed.): *Churches Respond to B E M*, Faith and Order Paper No. 111, Vol 3, p 65.
11. Minear, Paul: *Images of the Church in the New Testament*, Philadelphia, The Westminster Press, 1960.
12. Hill, Edmund: 'Church'. Komonchak, Joseph; Collins, Mary; Lane, Dermot A (eds.) *The New Dictionary of Theology*, Dublin, Gill and Macmillan, 1987, pp 185-201, p 189.
13. Schreiter, Robert: *Constructing Local Theologies*, London, S C M, 1985.
14. Schreiter: op cit supra (n 13), p 198.
15. Dulles, Avery: *Models of the Church*, Dublin, Gill & Macmillan, 1976. Robert Bellarmine's definition of Church 'was bought at a price,' p 14.

16. Schmaus: op cit supra (n 1), p 5.
17. Other instances are found in Abbott, op cit supra (n 2), *Lumen Gentium*, p 26, par 9, p 79, par 48.
18. Philips, Gerard: 'History of the Constitution'. Vorgrimler, Herbert (gen. ed.): *Commentary on the Documents of Vatican II*, Vol 1, W.Germany, Herder K G, 1967, pp 105-137, p 111.
19. Grillmeier, Aloys: 'Chapter 1'. Vorgrimler, op cit supra (n 18) 'Article 9:3 (*Lumen Gentium*) alludes to the words of St Cyprian which designate the Church as 'the invisible sacrament of unity,'' pp 138-152, p 140.
20. Rahner: op cit supra (n 7).
21. Schillebeeckx: op cit supra (n 8).
22. Rahner: op cit supra (n 7), p 14.
23. Rahner: op cit supra (n 7), p 16.
24. Boff, Leonardo: *Sacraments of Life and Life of the Sacraments*, Washington, Pastoral Press, 1987, p 31.
25. Houtepen: op cit supra (n 9). 'But a certain triumphalism and ecclesiological monophysitism looms behind all High Church ecclesiologies.' p 230.
26. Grillmeier: op cit supra (n 18), pp 147-8.
27. Schillebeeckx: op cit supra (n 8), p 47
28. Rahner: op cit supra (n 7), p 31.
29. Abbott: op cit supra (n 2), *Lumen Gentium*, p 79, par 48.
30. Moltmann, Jurgen: *The Trinity and the Kingdom of God*, London, S C M, 1981.
31. Boff, Leonardo: *Trinity and Society*, London, Burns and Oates, 1988. Moreover, this trinitarian approach is in tune with W.C.C.'s self-identity as expressed at New Delhi in 1961; see Vischer: op cit supra (n 24), pp 144-163.
32. Abbott: op cit supra (n 2), *Lumen Gentium*, p 22, par 8.
33. Abbott: op cit supra (n 2), *Lumen Gentium*, p 19, par 6.
34. ibid.
35. ibid.
36. Abbott: op cit supra (n 2), *Lumen Gentium*, p 20, par 6.
37. Grillmeier: op cit supra (n 18), p 141.
38. Abbott: op cit supra (n 2), *Lumen Gentium*, p 22, par 8.

39. Abbott, op cit supra (n 2), *Lumen Gentium*, p 26, par 9.
40. Abbott: op cit supra (n 2), *Lumen Gentium*, p 24, par 8.
41. Schillebeeckx, Edward: *The Mission of the Church*, London, Sheed and Ward, 1973, p 7. See also Arcic, *Salvation and the Church*, London, Church House, 1987. 'Yet, until the Kingdom is realised in its fullness, the Church is marked by human limitation and imperfection. It is the beginning and not yet the end, the first fruits and not yet the final harvest.' par 30.
42. Abbott: op cit supra (n 2), *Unitatis Redintegratio*, p 350, par 6.
43. Abbott: op cit supra (n 2), *Lumen Gentium*, p 22, par 8.
44. Abbott: op cit supra (n 2), *Lumen Gentium*, p 20, par 6.
45. Abbott: op cit supra (n 2), *Unitatis Redintegratio*, pp 341-366.
46. Abbott: op cit supra (n 2), *Unitatis Redintegratio*, p 346, par 3.
47. ibid. footnote 19.
48. Schillebeeckx: op cit supra (n 8), p 55.
49. Rahner: op cit supra (n7), p 20.
50. Abbott: op cit supra (n 2), *Ad Gentes*, p 590, par 5.
51. Falconer, Alan: 'The Ministry of the Whole People of God.' *Doctrine and Life* Vol 38, No 1, 1988, pp 20-28.
52. Abbott... op cit supra (n 2), *Lumen Gentium*, p 24, par 8. See also *Gaudium et Spes*, p 245, par 43; *Unitatis Redintegratio*, p 350, par 6.
53. Abbott: op cit supra (n 2), *Unitatis Redintegratio*, p 348, par 4.
54. Buthelezi, Manas: 'The Church as a Prophetic Sign'. Limouris, Gennadios: Faith and Order Paper No 130, Geneva, WCC, 1986, pp 138-144, p 140.
55. Abbott: op cit supra (n 2), *Lumen Gentium*, p 24, par 8.
56. Abbott: op cit supra (n 2), *Gaudium et Spes*, p 247 par 45. See also: 'Report of the First Consultation of the Unity/Renewal Study'. Limouris: op cit supra (n 54), p 173.
57. International Committee on English in the Liturgy, *The Roman Missal*, Dublin, Liturgical Books, 1974, Eucharistic-Prayer, No 4, p 504.
58. Bonhoeffer, Dietrich: 'Thy Kingdom Come'. Godsey, D: *Preface to Bonhoeffer*, Philadelphia, Fortress Press, 1965, p 28.

59. Schillebeeckx: op cit supra (n 8), p 48.
60. Semmelroth, Otto: 'Chapter 7'. Vorgrimler: op cit supra (n 18), p 282.
61. Abbott: op cit supra (n 2), *Lumen Gentium*, p 78, par 48.
62. Boff, Leonardo: *Ecclesiogenesis*, London, Collins, 1986.
63. Rahner, Karl: 'The Church and the Parousia of Christ', *Theological Investigations*, Vol.6, Baltimore, Helicon, 1969, pp 295-312, p 198.
64. Mc Brien, Richard P: *Do We Need the Church*, London, Collins,
65. Mc Donagh, Enda: *The Demands of Simple Justice*, Dublin, Gill and Macmillan, 1980. 'Absence of justice, truth,freedom and compassion in the church subject it to the condemnation of the kingdom and leave it in a very weak position to confront the wider society in the kingdom's name.' p 42.
66. Abbott: op cit supra (n 2), *Lumen Gentium*, p 79, par 48.
67. Abbott: op cit supra (n 2), *Lumen Gentium*, p 26, par 9.
68. Dulles: op cit supra (n 1), p 145.
69. Grillmeier: op cit supra (n 18), p 139.
70. Abbott... op cit supra (n 2), *Lumen Gentium*, p 24, par 8. See also 'Report of the First Consultation of the Unity/Renewal Study'. Limouris: op cit supra (n 56), p 173, par 48.
71. As we are not at the stage of W.C.C. bringing together the traditions of all those that contribute towards it, when we speak of a 'W.C.C. tradition' it is truer to understand it as being in addition to the already existing traditions.

CHAPTER 2

The Catholic Church's Response to the troubles in Northern Ireland

1. FOCUS

Considering the church as a sacrament for the world invites us towards contextualising the church. The word sacrament is generally understood to refer to the church's individual sacraments, each of which is a particular actualisation of the church's essential nature, proper to a specific setting and time. And so it is fitting to now consider the church as sacrament in a particular setting, since the church cannot avoid becoming involved with the particularities of each culture. The particular culture chosen here is that of Northern Ireland, but it is only as example, and I invite the reader to keep her or his own particular culture in mind. In this section I examine the official response of the Roman Catholic Church to the violence of the last twenty years, and consider to what extent that reflects the church as sacrament as outlined in chapter 1. As I am concentrating on the official response, I will take some examples of statements from the Conference of Bishops and of statements, talks and homilies from some of the individual bishops during that time. I suggest that a similar study of the stances of the other churches could profitably be done, drawing on statements from their spokespersons.

2. THE RESPONSE – PASTORAL?

(a) Condemnation as Primary

The single most obvious note struck in the vast majority of statements issued by the Catholic hierarchy,[1] collectively and individually, concerning the violence in Northern Ireland since 1968 is that of condemnation:

Our main purpose in this statement, however, is to repeat, unreservedly and without qualification, our condemnation of this campaign of violence.[2]

Since the present campaign of violence began it has been condemned over and over again by the Catholic bishops of Ireland. Once more we condemn it and express our horror at the deaths and terrible injuries inflicted on innocent people.[3]

The same strong theme of condemnation is to be seen in the statements of individual bishops. In fact, as early as 15 February 1971, Cardinal Conway claimed that he had already condemned violence twenty-three times since the outbreak began in August, 1968.[4] And the condemnations are wide-ranging, embracing the I.R.A. and all associating with the organisation, loyalist paramilitaries and the security forces.[5]

There is evidence that the bishops had reservations about both the nature and frequency of the condemnations, with Bishop Edward Daly saying: 'The vocabulary of condemnation and frustration is exhausted. Anything one can say has been said dozens of times already.'[6] Similar sentiments were expressed by the Irish Episcopal Conference[7] and probably informed Bishop Cahal Daly's[8] explicit move from condemnation to appeal in a number of his funeral homilies.[9] Yet condemnation remains the most constant feature of the statements from the bishops concerning Northern Ireland. For the most part, these do not accord with the description of condemnation given by Bishop Cahal Daly when he talked in August, 1976 as bishop of Ardagh and Clonmacnois:

It (moral condemnation) accepts the speaker's share of guilt for the circumstances in which the evil is done. The condemnation is uttered in awareness of one's own need for repentence and forgiveness. To have the right to utter moral condemnation, one must recognise one's own sinfulness.[10]

(In this description, Bishop Cahal Daly points in a direction that I intend to consider in later chapters.) Would some of the bishops' statements not come closer to what Bishop Cahal Daly speaks of as 'moralistic denunciation,' which is 'directed at the evildoer in person and tends to abound in language stressing his total exclusion from the society of the speaker.'?[11]

There is without question an obligation on the bishops to condemn evil. But it becomes questionable when, in the public perception, such condemnation appears to be mere ritual denunciation, the thing to be expected from a bishop.[12] What this can give rise to is a 'theology of the last atrocity,'[13] and a ministry of the last atrocity, where what is said is reactive in character, with little attention to analysis or reflection. Even though as early as 1971 the northern bishops said in a statement: 'On a future occasion we may find it necessary to speak at some length on some aspects of the present situation...'[14] we are still without any such treatment from that body.

In 1975 the hierarchy issued a Pastoral Letter called *Human Life is Sacred*.[15] This document deals with a wide range of 'life' issues from abortion to euthanasia, and includes christian teaching on education, family welfare and parenthood. It is in such a context that the topic of violence is taken up, and is given 8 paragraphs in a document of 127 paragraphs. The purpose of the 8 paragraphs is to alert 'consciences, especially those of our own flock, to evil.'[16] Its single focus is a refutation of the principle, the end justifies the means. The document does not attempt any theological analysis of violence or non-violence in the Irish context, but settles for general, and I think, over-simplified, statements such as: 'the theory of modern revolution is an extreme version of the philosophy that the end justifies the means;'[17] and again: 'modern revolutionary violence enshrines the evil philosophy that intentions are the sole determinant of the morality of actions.'[18]

It must be said that on a number of occasions Bishop Cahal Daly has analysed various aspects of the northern situation in talks and speeches he has delivered,[19] but the bishops have yet to address the matter of violence in a sustained and substantial fashion.

The bishops cannot be held totally responsible for the reactive and immediate nature of their contributions: 'Those statements and documents were initally expected and sought by the professional communicators and politicians.'[20] Bishop Edward Daly, who had voiced reservations about making public statements at the beginning of his episcopate,[21] was to come to a similar conclusion. In February 1985 he decided not to issue statements about violence in the course of his ordinary preaching:

> I do not intend to issue statements in future, at the behest of the media or anyone else, immediately after such atrocities have taken place... There is nothing new left to say. The vocabulary has been exhausted. It is my belief that the litany of condemnation is now hackneyed and totally predictable, and only serves to generate more publicity and media exposure for those who follow the vocation of murder.[22]

Statements of condemnation have indeed become less frequent from the bishops in recent years. But it would appear that such a move is tactical – less frequent condemnation in the hope that it might be more effective. Are there not theological and ecclesiological reasons for questioning, not the existence of condemnations, but the extent and tone of them when they become the major profile of the hierarchy? Jesus, who himself lived at a time of political turmoil, spoke words of condemnation[23] but could anyone say that it became his major profile? 'For God sent his Son into the world not to condemn the world, but so that through him the world might be saved.' (Jn 3:17) And he gave a warning against too ready condemnation: 'Take the plank out of your own eye first, and then you will see clear enough to take out the splinter that is in your brother's eye.' (Lk 6:42)

We can at times glimpse the possibility of such a self-questioning attitude in some of the statements from the bishops. Bishop Edward Daly said:

> Might I end this statement by quoting once again from Bishop Cahal Daly's speech in London: 'The christian cannot evade

the duty of moral vigilance or forget the Lord's injunction about the visual block in one's own eye.' This applies to all of us trapped in this situation which history has imposed on us.[24]

But such an attitude is quite rare and does not seem to have been sustained in any substantial way. I think this is a major criticism of the church's position and I will take up this issue later in chapter 3.

(b) Caring for the Distressed
In the statements from the hierarchy, especially in the sermons at funerals of victims of violence, it is clear that the bishops are very aware of the sufferings of the people: 'We call on all who are responsible for deeds of violence to gaze on the horrors they are causing and listen to the anguished cries of the dying and the maimed.'[25]

Bishop Edward Daly has made numerous statements concerning the distress and anguish caused to people of his diocese, whether it be by I.R.A. violence or intimidation,[26] or by the security forces.[27] At funerals Bishop Cahal Daly has spoken frequently out of the depths of his own pain and grief:

Is a murder becoming just another statistic of violence, today's news item, forgotten next week? Yet one has only to visit the home of a murder victim and kneel by the coffin to know that each death is unlike any other, each grief is special and personal and unique. One never gets used to the scene. Each rends the heart again.'[28]

I do not doubt the sincerity nor the commitment of the bishops to caring for the community. This has been confirmed over and over again through the years, not only in many public ways, e.g. the consistency of bishops' presence at funerals and wakes, but also in the quiet, private help innumerable individuals have received from them, e.g. financial assistance to move house, counselling through trauma, support when in prison. But at the very heart of such helping and pastoral concern lies a serious danger, that of becoming, or being seen as, a tribal chaplain.[29]

(c) The Trap of Tribal Chaplaincy

The image of two opposing tribes has often been used to depict the troubles in the North, the native Irish against the colonisers, stemming from the Ulster Plantation of 1609.[30] Here confessional identities were an extremely important feature in the hostility.[31] Foster, writing about Ireland just before the Famine, quotes from Thackeray's *Irish Sketch Book* of 1842: '...there are two truths, the Catholic truth and the Protestant truth.'[32] The same could be said of Ireland many years on each side of that date, a separate truth for each tribe. Each of the tribes finds one of the mainstays of identity in its religion[33] and out of such a situation it is almost inevitable that those who are seen as 'leaders' in the religious field will also be seen as leaders of the tribes, or tribal chaplains: '...we inherit a situation in which the Churches have acted as chaplains to two traditions which have been historically in conflict with each other.'[34]

The conflict has indeed polarised the two tribes who are now in a position, not only of opposition to each other, but where identity is formed and strengthened out of the very opposition itself. It is not simply that the separate identities have brought them into conflict, but the conflict itself is now core to their identities:

> The identity of each community has been shaped by the actions, attitudes and declarations of other communities. Both siege and coercion mentalities are reactions to the actions of others. The definition has been crafted over and against 'the other'.[35]

In such a situation it is almost impossible, when speaking from within one identity, to embrace those 'on the other side.' Instead of being religious leaders, such people becomes tribal spokespeople for their own communities.

This is not all negative. In being chaplains to their communities these leaders, both Catholic and Protestant, have been able to comfort, encourage, instruct, restrain and moderate the people.

Because of the close connection the Churches in Northern Ireland enjoy with their people they are inevitably identified with the needs and fears of those people. I recall many instances when the real presentations of the genuine fears of people have come from Church spokesmen alone. But there is all the difference in the world between identification and over-identification. Too often the integrity of the Christian voice has suffered because the voice of the Church has appeared to be over-identified with the feelings of one section of the community to the exclusion of everything else.[36]

I think there is an awareness of this problem among the church leaders in the North. In Bishop Edward Daly's first sermon as bishop he said: 'There is also the dilemma in which a bishop finds himself when called upon to comment. There is the fact that he has more responsibility for guiding his own flock than guiding others.'[37] (In the context of the North one could be excused for reading 'own tribe' for 'own flock.') Commenting on the situation, Robin Boyd says: 'But when it comes to the Irish situation, their concern (the Churches') – apart from a vague, general concern for peace – is primarily for members of their own community under pressure.'[38]

This ends up with the ridiculous yet tragic situation that the better the clergy of whatever denomination do their pastoral work, the more they play into the role of tribal chaplain and so reinforce the divisions in the community. The very worst expressions of this are vividly portrayed in the following passage from an address by Brian Walker, chairman of the New Ulster Movement, to the Irish Association of Priests:

Where but in Christian Ireland could murder and bloodshed be perpetrated day by day while church leaders, clerical and lay, wring their hands in pious horror but at the same time appear to offer excuses and explanations for the excesses of their adherents?[39]

We have examples of less dramatic expressions of tribal chaplaincy from the early days of the present troubles in statements from the bishops; for example, the way Cardinal Conway seems to exclude the Protestant community when speaking about a christian responsibility:

> The Catholic bishops have over and over again condemned killings and other forms of violence as a means to political ends, and it has been acknowledged that this view is shared by the great majority of *Catholic* people ... *Catholic* people should not allow themselves to be persuaded into violent or sterile self-destructive forms of protest.[40] (*italics, my addition*)

This is not to imply that the bishop cannot speak to or for 'his people'. It is inevitable that, being of a particular denomination, he will represent that group. That is how it should be and it seems to me that it happens throughout the world. There is nothing particularly Irish nor blameworthy about such an arrangement. But in the Irish situation, where tribalism is not only very deep but an active source of hostility in the community, tribal chaplaincy can go beyond representing particular groups and can become a focus of and an agent for polarisation, suspicion and even hatred. Moreover in Ireland, where exclusivity is so ingrained in the system and in peoples' hearts, tribal chaplaincy only confirms and reinforces this isolation. What is required from church people of every denomination is behaviour which would encourage inclusivity on all possible occasions:

> '...it (the voice of the church) must contain an objectivity and integrity which transcend sectional or denominational interest.'[41]

Bishop Cahal Daly speaks to this point when he says:

> I believe that churchmen must be careful not to speak to or for one political community only, but must endeavour to be aware of the impact which their words will have on the other political community as well. Churchmen must try to speak across the barriers dividing the two communities. No less is

demanded of the ministers of reconciliation which Christian pastors are called to be at all times, and particularly at this point in our history.[42]

And the same bishop challenges the existence and strength of the tribal ethos when he asks:

> I wonder how many of us, Catholic or Protestant, have ever found ourselves instinctively feeling that a Catholic or Protestant has betrayed the Church or compromised the faith when he or she chooses, if a Catholic, not to be a nationalist, or, if a Protestant, not to be a unionist?[43]

3. THE RESPONSE – ESCHATOLOGICAL?

As it is at present in Northern Ireland, the primary means of identity is that of denomination, which is, as we have seen, a breeding ground for exclusivism and sectarianism.[44] This can lead to opposition and hostility as members of each denomination sharpen their identity over against that of 'the other side', with each believing the truth to be theirs. There is little mobility or flexibility possible, with any move toward compromise open to be interpreted as either betrayal or take-over, depending on where one is standing. It is an understatement to say that in such a situation ecumenical contact does not come naturally or easily.[45] Bishop Cahal Daly addresses this matter when he says: 'We Catholic Bishops and priests have, I fear, in our pastoral practice, not always given ecumenism the priority our Church assigns to it...'[46] We hear the same sentiments spoken more sharply and severely by Michael Hurley S.J.:

> Certainly the resources so far committed to ecumenism, especially by contrast with other aspects of Church renewal, are so insignificant that we may say, with apologies to Chesterton, that 'ecumenism hasn't really failed; it simply hasn't been properly tried.'[47]

Ecumenism is not simply about Catholics and Protestants coming to understand the teachings of each other's church, nor is it about church leaders meeting in conference or speaking on the media. While all such activities may be positive contributions toward bridge building, what is required is a new way of people understanding who they are, where identity is not so totally locked into the denominational system. All christian churches have such a perspective available to them at the very heart of their self-understanding, as churches on pilgrimage, on their way to the God who 'transcends their ways of acting and their articulations of the nature of God and of the Church.'[48]

The church can be truly church only by being alive to and engaging with the eschatological dimension of its nature and purpose: 'Rather the eschatological outlook is characteristic of all christian proclamation, of every christian existence and of the whole church.'[49] Such a church would see itself as relative, here to serve the kingdom rather than as an end in itself. It would entail viewing itself as secondary, with confessional identity as provisional. It would aim at being truly catholic, universal and inclusive in the way Jesus was in his mission and person. It would offer people an identity and self-worth that are ultimately sought not in a political but in an eschatological context, where people would understand themselves as pilgrims on the way rather than as tribes threatened by anyone other than those of 'their own sort', a view of church current among many Catholics and Protestants in the North.

In studying the various statements of the bishops one gets little flavour of such a vision. One has the sense that they are very preoccupied (and it would be hard not to be) with the immediate pastoral situation e.g. the aftermath of a bombing or killing. In this setting the eschatological finds expression quite appropriately as pastoral support, in words of encouragement and in a call for perseverance and hope:

> Our religion is forever a religion of resurrection, of un-defeatable strength, of unshakeable hope. Christ has con-

quered death and the devil and sin and hell. Those who love
him can never give in to fear or despair or failure.[50]

On one or two other occasions we get a hint of what a strong
eschatological perspective on the troubles might have us consider:

being a Sign of the Kingdom means in part that we work for
new political structures in Northern Ireland in which the
identity of both nationalists and unionists is respected and
in which neither one can dominate the other.[51]

Such a sacramental and eschatological view of the church needs
much teasing out and practical application. What does it mean in
ecumenical terms to work for the kingdom here and now? What is
the meaning of the kingdom values of peace, justice and freedom
in Northern Ireland? What would reflection on the kingdom yield
by way of non-violent alternatives? 'There must be a vision before
there can be satisfactory action ... vision-forming is a necessary
stage on the road to political improvement.'[52] There is little evidence of anything like this being searched out.

Very rarely do we see the rich eschatological perspective explored
for its potential to inspire towards creative community building.
Could it be that such questions asked above, and the vision behind
them, might challenge the bishops to think in terms of pilgrim
rather than resident, where they would have to allow for their
'vision of truth' to be 'expanded and corrected by other people'?[53]
Could this have uncomfortable implications for the denominational leaders, the tribal chaplains?

4. THE RESPONSE – CHRISTOLOGICAL?

Christians in Ireland have not allowed the person and the
message of Jesus Christ challenge their sectarian viewpoint
and the gospel message is obscured by our sectarianism.[54]

While the above quotation applies to all the denominations, with
reference to the Roman Catholic Church it is worth asking about
the christological aspect of the church as seen from what the bish-

ops have been saying? Certainly the words of Christ are constantly spoken by them as they bring compassion and support to the bereaved and point the congregations beyond immediate thoughts of retaliation:

> If you are bringing your gifts to the altar and there you remember that your brother has something against you, leave your offering there before the altar, go and be reconciled with your brother first, and then come back and present your offering.(Mt 5:23-4)[55]

And again:

> Father, forgive them; they do not know what they are doing.'(Lk 23:34)[56]

These indeed are the words of Jesus, but which of the gospel images of Christ seem to predominate? As I have mentioned there is the caring, compassionate Christ, the forgiving Christ, the loving Christ. But it is always the Christ in charge, the Christ in control, the Christ who knows what to do and who moves forward without hesitation. What about the fearful, hesitant, frightened Christ; the Christ who was forced to examine the style of his own ministry through the temptations; the Christ who was confused about what exactly his Father was asking of him, and who on the cross seemed to come close to losing his nerve, and his faith, in the face of his approaching death? And what about the Christ who 'did not cling to his equality with God but emptied himself to assume the condition of a slave... ' (Phil 2:6-7) – the kenotic Christ, the servant Christ?

A christologically aware church, appropriate to the North, would need to give quite particular attention to the servant Christ, because of the perceived power of the Catholic church. 'There remains ... a deep-seated distrust of the Roman Catholic Church, not only in its doctrines but also in its power structures.'[57] We may have reassurances from the bishops to the contrary: 'The Catholic church in Ireland has no power and seeks no power except the power of the gospel it preaches...'[58] But many would challenge this opinion: 'The Roman Catholic Church, however, representing 96 per cent of the population, has exercised a great deal of pressure on the state, and continues to do so, though today in less obvious ways than before.'[59] It is out of such an understanding that Enda McDonagh says: '...it is more than time for them (the Irish Churches) to transform the self-serving picture of the servant Church and so of its servant leader, Jesus Christ, which is so readily, however mistakenly, perceptible to observers today.'[60]

One could surmise that it is out of a self-understanding of the church as powerful that the hierarchy has issued so many statements of condemnation, particularly early on in the troubles. Power in itself, of course, is not negative, but is simply the ability to influence people and acts. But there is a long tradition in church and state of power being used to enforce the will of these bodies, unilateral power, which, according to Loomer, 'operates so as to make the other a function of one's ends...'[61] Its outcome is polarisation and its currency often condemnation. This is a long way from the servant leadership of Jesus, whose power was a vulnerable power, the power of being powerless, the way of the suffering servant.

Finally, regarding the quotation from Paul O'Leary,O.P., opening this section, how are the bishops touched by the radical Christ, who, as Jew, broke through the barriers of his own religious identity over and over again? We see Jesus speaking to the Samaritan, spending time with the outcast and praising faith in the foreigner. He had the courage to move beyond traditions of his own time that many of the religious officials held as sacred, e.g. his attitude to the sabbath. Jesus's example was a challenge to life interpreted in a narrow denominational way, a challenge to the racist and exclusivist elements in his own tradition. It is now a challenge to our sectarian way and our tribal tradition.

In summary, then, from the analysis of the bishops' statements it is clear that they see it as part of their pastoral role to attend to the immediate suffering and brokenness of their congregations. But without doubt their primary profile has emerged from their statements of condemnation, and this has led to a sense of negativity being associated with how the church is perceived. While condemnation has a place in leadership, the warning against evil needs to be in the context of guiding and inspiring toward good. And this is where lack of attention to the christological and the eschatological has weakened the presence of the church as sacrament. The church has been captive to the pastoral demand of the present moment and so has neglected to call on the eschatalogical potential to be found within its own identity. Could it be that it is not only in Northern Ireland that the past and the present seem to be so overpowering that the church does not seem able to free itself toward vision and possibility for the future? And while the Christ it portrays is the Christ who comforts, little is seen of the suffering servant, aware of his own need and vulnerability. Nor is there much evidence of the boundary-breaking Christ, so badly needed to help free the church from the worst results of tribal chaplaincy. The church that emerges is an impoverished sacrament of Christ, and has left largely undiscovered the considerable potential of its sacramental nature to address the situation. Chapter 3 will consider how the church might see itself as sacrament in a way that would enable it to avail of this sacramental potential.

Notes

1.   There does not exist any official comprehensive collection of statements from the hierarchy. But an unofficial compilation of extracts from statements made by Cardinal Conway 1968-1972, who at that time often issued statements on behalf of the hierarchy, was made available to me by the Catholic Press and Information Office in Dublin. I have also studied all the major statements made by the Conference of Bishops on the northern violence since the recent outbreak in 1968. (See Bibliography)
2.   Joint statement by the Roman Catholic Bishops of Northern Ireland, 12 September, 1971.
3.   Statement by the Irish Bishops, 24 February, 1978.

4. Gallagher, Eric and Worrall, Stanley: *Christians in Ulster 1968-1980*, London, Oxford University Press, 1982, p 60.
5. See Bishop Edward Daly's homily at the funeral of Judge Rory Conaghan, 18 September, 1974.
    See also Bishop Cahal Daly's homily at the funeral of John O' Neill, 18 March, 1986; and the statement issued by the Northern Catholic Bishops, 4 July, 1983.
6. Statement issued by Bishop Edward Daly, 18 November, 1981.
7. Statement issued by the Irish Episcopal Conference, 9 November, 1987.
8. I refer to him as Bishop as that was his office at the time of the homilies and statements which I quote.
9. Bishop Cahal Daly's homily at the funeral of Miss Mary Travers, 11 April, 1984; and Bishop Cahal Daly's address at a service in St Anne's Cathedral, 16 March, 1987.
10. Interview with James Downey, Irish Times, 16 August, 1976.
11. ibid.
12. Draft Document issued by Catholic Institute of International Relations, London, 1987, pp 2,3.
13. Draft Document, op cit supra (n 12), p 3.
14. Joint Statement by the Roman Catholic Bishops of Northern Ireland, 12 September, 1971.
15. Irish Catholic Bishops: *Justice, Love and Peace, Pastoral Letters of the Irish Bishops*, 1969-1979, Dublin, Veritas, 1979.
16. Irish Catholic Bishops, *Human Life is Sacred*. Irish Catholic Bishops, op cit supra (n 15), pp 81-138, pp 112-3.
17. Irish Catholic Bishops: op cit supra (n 15), p 112.
18. Irish Catholic Bishops: op cit supra (n 15), p 114.
19. For example: Daly, Cahal: *Communities without Consensus*, Dublin, Irish Messenger Publications, 1985; see also Daly, Cahal: *Northern Ireland: Risk and Opportunity for the Churches*. Address at a Conference on the Role of the Churches in British-Irish Relationships, Dublin, 26 Nov., 1985.
20. Gallagher and Worrall: op cit supra (n 4), p 203.
21. Bishop Edward Daly's homily in St.Eugene's Cathedral,

1 April, 1974: '... It is a pity that condemnation has to be predominant.'

22. Statement issued by Bishop Edward Daly, 25 February, 1985.
23. Jesus attacks the lawyers and Pharisees: Lk 11:37-54.
24. Bishop Edward Daly's statement on his visit to Long Kesh Prison, 27 April, 1978.
25. Statement by Irish Bishops, 24 February, 1978.
26. Bishop Edward Daly's homily at the funeral of Sheila Lewis and Sean Dalton, 3 September, 1988.
27. Statement issued by Bishop Edward Daly, 17 January, 1977.
28. Bishop Cahal Daly's homily at the funeral of Malachy Trainor, 17 May, 1989.
29. Morrow, John: *Northern Ireland – A Challenge to Theology*, University of Edinburgh Centre for Theology and Public Issues, Occasional Paper No.12, 1987.
    Other references are: Boyd, Robin: *Ireland, Christianity Discredited or Pilgrim's Progress?*, Geneva, W.C.C., 1988, pp 50,51.
    See also Falconer, Alan: 'Remembering.' Studies, Vol 78 No 310, 1989, pp 169-176, p 171.
30. Darby, John: *Conflict in Northern Ireland*, Dublin, Gill and Macmillan. 'The deep resentment of the native Irish towards the planters, and the distrustful siege mentality of the planters towards the Irish, is the root of the Ulster problem.' p 3.
    See also Foster, Roy: *Modern Ireland 1600-1972*, London, Penguin Press, 1988, pp 59-78.
31. Lyons, F.S.L.: *Culture and Anarchy in Ireland 1890-1939*, Oxford, Oxford University Press, 1979, p 117. See also Hickey, John: *Religion and the Northern Ireland Problem*, Dublin, Gill and Macmillan, 1984, p 66.
32. Foster: op cit supra (n 30), p 319.
33. Morrow, John: 'The Captivity of the Irish Churches'. Audenshaw Papers No.45. '...the majority of church leaders and members have become captive to the political ideologies of Unionism or Nationalism...' p 1.

34. Morrow… op cit supra (n 33), p 14. See also O'Brien, C.C.:
    States of Ireland, London Hutchinson, 1972; he writes of the
    role of the churches in the North as 'encouraging, exalting
    and extending the kind of tribal-sectarian self-righteousness
    which forms a culture in which so easily multiplies.' p 312.
35. Falconer… op cit supra (n 29), p 171.
36. Eames, Robin: The Future: *The Contribution of the Irish
    Churches I*: Hanna, Eamon (ed): Reconciliation in Northern
    Ireland, Social Study Conference 1987, Belfast, Social Studies
    Conference Publications, p 66.
37. Bishop Edward Daly's homily in St Eugene's Cathedral, 1
    April, 1974.
38. Boyd: op cit supra (n 29), p 51.
39. Gallagher and Worrall: op cit supra (n 4), p 72.
40. Statement by Cardinal Conway, 14 August, 1971.
41. Eames: op cit supra (n 36), p 64.
42. Bishop Cahal Daly's homily at the funeral of Martin Duffy,
    22 July, 1986.
43. Daly, Cahal: *Northern Ireland: Risk and Opportunity for the
    Churches*. Address at a Conference on The Role of the
    Churches in British-Irish Relationships, Dublin, 26 Nov.,
    1985,
44. Darby: op cit supra (n 30). 'A more serious charge is that all
    the major Irish churches have used their influence, where
    possible, to enforce a sectarian ethos on the general
    community.' p 136.
45. Mc Evoy, James: 'Theology and the Irish Future: Viewpoint
    of a Northern Catholic'. Mc Donagh, Enda (ed.): *Irish Chal-
    lenges to Theology*, Dublin, Dominican Publications, 1986,
    pp 21-41.
46. Daly, Cahal: *Northern Ireland: Risk and Opportunity for the
    Churches*. Address at a Conference on The Role of the
    Churches in British-Irish Relationships, Dublin, 26 Nov.,
    1985,

47. Hurley, Michael: *The Future: The Contribution of the Christian Churches II*: Hanna, Eamon (ed.): op cit supra (n 36), pp 69-80, p 73.
48. Falconer, Alan: 'The Churches: Pilgrims or Residents?' *Doctrine and Life*, Vol 40 No 1 January 1990, pp 4-10, p 5.
49. Moltmann, Jurgen: *The Theology of Hope*, London, S C M, 1967, p 16
50. Bishop Cahal Daly's homily at the funeral of Colum McCallan, 18 July, 1986.
51. Bishop Cahal Daly's homily in St Peter's Pro-Cathedral, 27 October, 1985.
52. Daly, Gabriel: 'Towards an Irish Theology: Some Questions of Method.' Mc Donagh (ed.): op cit supra (n 45), pp 88-101, pp 95, 6.
53. Falconer: op cit supra (n 48), p 5.
54. O'Leary, Paul: 'Christology and the Conflict in Ireland.' Milltown Studies, No.9, August 1982, pp1-14, p 12.
55. Bishop Cahal Daly's homily at the funeral of Martin Duffy, 22 July, 1986.
56. Bishop Cahal Daly's homily at the funeral of Martin Quinn, 1 February, 1986.
57. Gallagher and Worrall: op cit supra (n 4), p 53.
58. Irish Episcopal Conference Delegation, *New Ireland Forum, Report of Proceedings*, 9 February, 1984, Dublin, Stationary Office, 1984, p 2.
59. Boyd: op cit supra (n 29), p 99. See also Mc Sweeney, Bill. 'Religious Dimensions of the Troubles in Northern Ireland.' Draft paper for publication in *Religion, State and Society in Modern Britain*, Dublin, Macmillan, 1987, pp 1-17, pp 13,4.
60. Mc Donagh, Enda: *Doing the Truth*, Dublin, Gill and Macmillan, 1979, p 161.
61. Loomer, Bernard: 'Two Kinds of Power'. *Criterion*, Union of Chicago Divinity School, Vol 15 No 1, pp 11-29, p 14.

CHAPTER 3

Saving Suspicion

1. THE ROLE OF INTERPRETATION

In the previous chapter I have looked at how the bishops are addressing the northern violence out of their understanding of their role and the situation. But since 'to understand at all is to interpret,'[1] what we have seen is their interpretation. Does it all then come down to interpretation? What about the truth of the situation? We have already a response to this question in the quotation from Thackeray: 'There are two truths, the Catholic truth and the Protestant truth;'[2] – an acknowledgement of the place of interpretation, however primitive!

Now I will look briefly at the study of interpretation (hermeneutics) and then explore a particular strand of interpretation – 'interpretation as exercise of suspicion'[3] – and discuss what this can reveal. Then I will examine how this particular approach to interpretation is found in the Judaeo-Christian tradition, has a place today in the church, and in the very notion of sacrament. The work of David Tracy[4] will be particularly helpful in this exploration.

When Tracy addresses the notion of truth he says: 'Truth is the reality we know through our best interpretations.'[5] For him, to live in any sort of human way at all involves interpretation. But there are particular times when 'older ways of understanding and practice, even experience itself, no longer seem to work.'[6] At times like that – and who would doubt that we now live in such times in Northern Ireland? – we need to examine closely the way we interpret events, reactions and traditions.

For Tracy there is no single, sacred understanding or interpretation of events, but a struggle to interpret through our history, culture, society and language. Gone are the days of the single certainty and what we now seek is 'relative adequacy,'[7] relative to our ability to listen and understand, relative to what is disclosed to us in a particular culture and at a particular time. Nothing is quite what it appears to be. The very language we use no longer can be understood as a tool, in the instrumental sense, enabling us to comprehend some objective reality, but rather: 'it is always there, surrounding and invading all I experience, understand, judge, decide, and act upon. I belong to my language far more than it belongs to me...'[8]

The same can be said of history; we can shape history, but equally so, or even more so, we are shaped by it. And it is now acknowledged that history is not a matter of a simple narrative of how things took place. There are different histories of the same event.[9] There is a number of reasons for this: firstly, history itself is ambiguous. Just as there is no single, simple certainty, neither is there any single, simple event: 'Every great work of civilisation is at the same time a work of barbarism.'[10] What was progress for the American whites was oppression for the blacks. There is ambiguity at the very heart of history. And secondly, in speaking or writing about any event we are speaking or writing about ourselves; the four evangelists give us four versions of the single life-event of Jesus of Nazareth, each according to the author's particular purpose, and historical, cultural and social context. And again, there is a Catholic and a Protestant version of the history of Northern Ireland, and within each there are many versions of the same event or period. A very important reason for such differences is, according to Tracy, the presence in each one of us of 'ideology.'[11]

To explain what he means by this term, Tracy draws on his understanding of the notion of 'sin,' this being different from error or mistake in that it operates at a deeper level in our being. It is something that de-centres the very self, and it is named by Tracy as 'radical alienation or systematic distortion.'[12] Because of it we can delude ourselves at very deep levels, even without being conscious of it happening. While all appears to be fine on the ordinary conscious level of living and rationality, there are forces within us distorting our perception for all sorts of selfish or sinful reasons.[13] So ambiguity belongs to the human condition itself because of the 'radical otherness'[14] that exists at the very centre of our being. And according to Tracy the way to hear this radical otherness is through a 'hermeneutic of suspicion'.[15] I will now take each of these concepts, first the hermeneutic of suspicion (since this is the tool) and then otherness, (the outcome of suspicion) and explore their meaning. Following this, I will consider the contribution these concepts can make to the understanding of sacrament.

2. HERMENEUTICS OF SUSPICION

(a) Saving Suspicion

A hermeneutic of suspicion invites us, not just to think, or even think twice, before we speak, but to examine the very thinking process, so that what we eventually think and say will be 'relatively adequate,' or relatively free from conscious and un-conscious distortion. It alerts us to the presence of self-interest and challenges us to remove this element inasmuch as we can become aware of it. It is, as Ricoeur says: 'doubting the consciousness with the aim of extending it.'[16] In these terms suspicion is a process, with other people in turn and in time becoming suspicious of what we say and do. Therefore, while being radically critical, it is essentially constructive and hope making. I am reminded of what Metz speaks of when he talks of a bad conscience: 'It is the courage to have a bad conscience, and the perseverance not to allow oneself to be talked out of it, that may be the only way today to have a conscience at all.'[17]

Tracy refers the reader to Paul Ricoeur and his book, *Freud and Philosophy*,[18] as his source for the notion of a hermeneutic of suspicion. There Ricoeur names Marx, Nietzsche and Freud as the three masters who dominate the school of suspicion, and who, although different in many ways, come together in their perception of 'the truth as lying.'[19] Coming from different directions they each attack the claims of conscious rationality; they say that there is no such thing as the simple truth. Marx suspects that the conscious truth is distorted by unrecognised motivations of socio-economic forces. Nietzsche suspects distortion through the desire for power, latent in whatever we say and do. And Freud uncovers the conscious as distorted at its very core through the drives, energies and repressions that exist in all our unconscious.[20] Nothing indeed is as it appears. 'We are,' says Nietzsche, 'in the phase of the modesty of consciousness.'[21]

Because of these suspicions the three masters saw the whole of consciousness primarily as 'false' consciousness. It is as if consciousness is trying to defraud us, and we can move beyond this only by taking this into account, seeking out the unconscious motivations and re-reading the conscious in that light. 'Guile will be met by double guile,'[22] consciousness extended through suspicion. The notion of suspicion, which in common parlance is such a negative term, is here used with a positive intent, suspicion that clarifies,[23] and hence saving suspicion. I name it 'saving' because it reveals, and can save us from, our distortions that arise from the unconscious wherein resides our radical otherness. The term 'saving' has also got Christian overtones, and I intend to go on to show how suspicion can save or redeem us. Moreover, it is only those who are saved – trusting and hopeful in their belief – who can have the inner freedom and courage to be suspicious. Lastly, using suspicion in the way intended, saves suspicion itself from being only a divisive force as it has become so tragically in Northern Ireland.

(b) Otherness
This concept of otherness and the Other is being addressed by some of the greatest philosophers of this century.[24] It is also a theme in religious and theological studies.[25] Rudolf Otto, in his book, *The Idea of the Holy*,[26] analyses the nature of holiness – which has the Hebrew root 'kds', meaning separate or apart – and comes up with the term 'numinous'[27] to describe the mysterious quality

of the divine. The numinous he calls 'wholly other.' We are engaged in a dialectic in our response to this 'wholly other.'[28] We feel it to be fearful and attractive at the same time. It is *tremendum et fascinans*,[29] and we are both repelled and attracted. These two movements exist at the same time and we negate the deity if we imagine that we can in any way dismantle this ambiguity.

I suggest that the radical otherness, not only around but within, is some reflection of Otto's 'wholly other'. Among that which is 'other around' is the stranger, the one different from me. God, the holy one, the totally other, creates all human beings in the divine image and in so doing shares this holiness or otherness. It is as if this characteristic of otherness, which marks the uniqueness, individuality and mystery of each person is a spark of the divine in each created being. But in situations of threat, especially of violence, we find it difficult to sustain the ambiguity of fear and attraction that rightly belong to this other, the stranger, and so we simplify matters for ourselves by concentrating on only that which is fear-making in the other. The 'other within', on which I will mainly focus, refers to that which is hidden, the unconscious, 'the other person in us'[30] and here the temptation is to neglect or ignore this other because of its potential to cause fear and disturbance. So, for our seeming security and safety, in an effort to manage the anxiety and threat we feel, we emphasise the fearful in the other around – the stranger – and disown the fearful in the other within – the unconscious.

It is relatively simple for us to be alert to what is going on in our conscious minds but it is when we risk being open to conscious and unconscious alike that a more complete awareness is possible. According to Tracy: '...the most radical otherness is within. Unless we acknowledge that, it will be impossible for us to responsibly participate in, or meaningfully belong to, our history.'[31] And when we begin to hear the otherness in ourselves, 'what we might then begin to hear, above our own chatter, are possibilities we have never dared to dream.'[32] The source of vision is the radical other within.

This other within has been named 'shadow'[33] or the dark side of our nature. Unfortunately this can be heard perjoratively and be associated with sin, whereas the shadow or darkness refers more properly to the hidden and unknown quality of the unconscious. (Sin can enter when we ignore its presence, or engage with the unconscious without the restraints and controls afforded by the conscious.) Therein are the 'dark' recesses of our being, which are difficult to plumb, uncomfortable, disturbing, not always immediately understood when accessed, and which forever complicate the one dimensional type of living that consciousness alone provides. Not only do consciousness and unconsciousness need each each other, as the light needs the dark, but each actually implies 'the other'; they can exist only in togetherness. To live in awareness and with responsibility we need to have the courage to embrace the conscious and unconscious alike.

(c) Relation between Saving Suspicion and Otherness

Because of the hidden character of the unconscious it is there that distortion can take place, and where things can go 'fundamentally and systematically awry in our history.'[34] It is from there that distortion can wield its destructive power, and all the more deadly through us being unaware of its presence. To alert us to such possibility, and to minimise the danger of us deluding ourselves at a level more fundamental than any conscious error, we call on the strategy named hermeneutic of suspicion, 'doubting our consciousness with the aim of extending it.'[35] Through this practice we are enabled to uncover, to a degree that is 'relatively adequate', some of the layers of our unconscious motivations, 'to face the actuality of ideologies in ourselves,'[36] and then take these forces into account as we consider what to do or say next.

Without this otherness of the unconscious being uncovered or acknowledged, what we are left with is the dullness and deadness of 'more of the same';[37] no movement, no new thoughts, no new ground broken. Suspicion brings us to the realm of new understandings. There is no thing that does not possess some element of otherness, yet the temptation is to domesticate reality and to 'force it into the Procrustean bed of more of the same,'[38] because there is no threat where there is sameness. We may deaden ourselves to the presence of otherness but that in no way lessens its existence. It is through saving suspicion that we are released into a relatively adequate awareness of this other that exists within in the unconscious which is the seed-bed of ideology, and which, unknown to us, informs our attitudes and behaviours.

If this other within is not acknowledged then we can so easily end up with singleminded fanaticism or fundamentalism, and the 'righteous purity of a siege mentality where we alone possess the truth.'[39] Or else we will engage in what is known as projection.

While this psychological theory was initially proposed in relation to individuals, it is also applicable to groups, organisations and even to states.[40] It claims that whatever feelings – usually difficult and uncomfortable – we are unable to admit or face up to in ourselves are projected onto another who is then experienced as possessing these feelings and may be blamed for expressing them. Others are blamed or punished for what we have been unable or unwilling to face up to in ourselves. It is suspicion that enables us to take responsibility for what is happening within ourselves, and to truly own the fearful, the disturbing and the difficult that is genuinely ours. According to Jung:

> Nothing has a more divisive and alienating effect upon society than this moral complacency and lack of responsibility, and nothing promotes understanding and rapprochement more than the mutual withdrawal of projections. This necessary corrective requires self-criticism, for one cannot just tell the other person to withdraw them...We can recognise our prejudices and illusions only when, from a broader psychological knowledge of ourselves and others, we are prepared to doubt the absolute rightness of our assumptions...'[41]

3. PLACE FOR SUSPICION OR SELF-CRITICISM

(a) In the Judaeo-Christian Tradition

The hermeneutic of suspicion has a pedigree within the Judaeo-Christian tradition that stretches as far back as the prophets, people who served Yahweh and their community by being critical of false religion that appeared to some people as the truth and as from Yahweh.

> The prophets of Israel offer us a detailed critical description of the corrupting religious trends; we learn from them to distinguish idolatrous religion, superstition, hypocrisy, legalistic religion, and finally religion as source of group-egotism and collective blindness.[42]

Many of these prophets operated from 'within the established power structure'[43] of the religious world of the day. They did not just stand at a safe distance and point out the wrong-doings of the people or the priests, but rather worked from within the system to encourage loyalty towards Yahweh. Isaiah and Jeremiah are specially noteworthy in this regard. At the time of both these prophets (Isaiah 765-c700, Jeremiah 646-c575) the monarchy was generally seen to have been an instrument of the covenant between Yahweh and his people. Through the covenant and by means of the kingship, Yahweh's peace and justice would be established throughout the land.

There existed at this time court prophets in the service of the king and these men were advisors regarding policy and tactics. From the evidence we have from Scripture, it appears that Isaiah belonged to the court and while he was in favour of the monarchy we find him being critical of particular kings and their policies. His opposition to Ahaz is especially forthright, firstly in private (Is 7:17-25) and then in public. (Is 8:5f.) Although in favour of the office he is harshly critical of the office-holder. The same can be said of Jeremiah. In a few chapters (Jer 21,22) we have a collection of prophecies against a number of kings – Zedekiah, Jehoickim, Jehoiakim. The people under these kings had abandoned Yahweh, so now Yahweh would abandon them. Jeremiah even went so far as to encourage his fellow countrymen to desert (Jer 22:9) which could be seen as the vilest act of treachery, preaching against king and nation, and yet this was a saving act and an expression of Jeremiah's loyalty to Yahweh, to the monarchy and most immediately to his own people.

Moreover, while the prophet is commonly associated with the future, in ways the truth is quite opposite to that. What was important for him was the history of Yahweh's self-revelation to his people through e.g. the Exodus and the Covenant. The prophet's task was to call people back to be faithful to this presence of Yahweh, to his word and his will for the people Israel. The people had abandoned their identity that had been established by Yahweh; they were now to be saved and called back to their God. So essentially, the prophets carried nothing new to the people. They addressed them from within their own tradition, recalling what was most sacred therein, and urged the people to make room in their lives for the God of such holy things and sacred ways. In summing up the work of the prophets Power says:

> The prophets preached nothing radical or revolutionary. Rather they tried to recall Israel to the old themes and the old truths – to the memory of the exodus and God's guiding care in the desert, to Sinai and the Decalogue, to the early days when Yahweh was their God but they were really his people. They pointed how far Israel had wandered from her historical mission as the people of Yahweh...'[44]

(b) In Church
But the Christian church, even more than Israel before it, showed itself unwilling to listen to this aspect of the presence of Yahweh inviting self-criticism. Different forms of ideology – distortion in the service of self-interest – got in the way and from the very beginning we see expressions of this: as a form of self-protection the critical preaching of Jesus – his denunciation of legalism, hypocrisy and collective blindness – was projected by the early church onto

the Jews, the scribes, Pharisees and temple priests. Then as the church became established and aligned itself with the secular powers, religion strengthened itself as a 'world maintaining' rather than a 'world shaking'[45] force, and largely abandoned the self-critical dimension.

Yet at the very heart of Christianity is the dynamic of resistance in the shape of Jesus on the cross, challenging the religious and secular powers of his day, and challenging also our human condition with his paradoxes: lose life to save it; (Mt 10:39) grain of wheat dies before the rich harvest; (Jn 12:24) first will be last and last first; (Mt 19:30) and above all, life through death. All these are expressions of things being other than they appear to be, of ambiguity being at the heart of all that is.

It must be acknowledged therefore that ambiguity exists at the heart of religion itself. Christianity teaches that we are vulnerable to sin and open to selfishness and self-interest. Because such is the human condition, then this must be as true in relation to our dealings with religious matters as with secular affairs. Christianity tells us in many ways to suspect the world, using the standards and values of the kingdom, but it cannot preach such a message without applying it to itself:

> Absence of justice, truth, freedom and compassion in the
> church subject it to the condemnation of the kingdom and
> leave it in a very weak position to confront the wider society
> in the kingdom's name.[46]

The church itself, therefore, must listen to this message and not just preach it to others. The word of prophecy, in fact, is always addressed first to the community of faith, and that is where the judgement of God begins. Could then Freud and Marx be seen as prophets?

> ...the great critics of religion, Ludwig Feuerbach, Karl Marx
> or Sigmund Freud, however much we may disagree with
> their premises, function as iconoclasts, challenging the
> church to examine its life and witness.[47]

It can be a very difficult task for any institution, for any church, to be self-critical, and maybe quite particularly for the Catholic Church, with the tradition of certainty and the influence of infallibility being very strong in the minds of the people.[48] It is not a church that is easily 'prepared to doubt the absolute rightness of (its) own assumptions.'[49] In the face of criticism, no matter how benign the intent, the fear can be that authority and power might be undermined, confidence weakened, failure exposed. How then can suspicion and church exist together? Uneasily, must be the answer. It was so in the time of the prophets, and it cannot now be any different. And it is not unknown for the church to adopt an oppressive stance toward those offering criticism, with theologians being ordered to withdraw comment and promise silence. Criticism in this perspective is seen as betrayal, the accusation made in regards to Jeremiah.

> ...because of the Church's power structure, critics, however commited to their faith and discreet in their criticism, are treated as suspect and disloyal, and excluded from opportunities and positions in the Church in which they might usefully contribute.[50]

And yet there is acknowledgement in Vatican II that:

> Christ summmons the Church, as she goes her pilgrim way, to that continual reformation of which she always has need, insofar as she is an institution of men *and women* here on earth. Therefore, if the influence of events or the times has led to deficiencies in conduct, in Church discipline, or even in the formulation of doctrine (which must be carefully distinguished from the deposit itself of faith), these should be appropriately rectified at the proper moment.[51] (italics, my addition)

This openness to reformation is a call by the church to attend to itself in a spirit of suspicion, towards ongoing self-correcting. Since such suspicion is under the guidance of the Holy Spirit,[52] it can truly be named saving suspicion. It appears, therefore, that saving suspicion is essential for the wellbeing of the church, a suspicion that can be saving for the world and also for itself, a spirit of critical discernment that helps the church increase in 'fidelity to her own calling.'[53]

If the church were to close itself to this other within then all it could do would be to reproduce itself – more of the same. In otherness and difference reside the potential to energise the church for its pilgrim way, for ecclesiogenesis. Although this is not stated as such in Vatican II, it is clearly the assumption behind what is probably the most discussed sentence of the entire Council. By saying that the 'Church ... subsists in the Catholic Church,'[54] and is not simply to be identified with the Roman Catholic Church, it is acknowledged that what is other than the Roman Catholic Church possesses 'many elements of sanctification and of truth,'[55] is used by the Holy Spirit as 'means of salvation,'[56] and so contributes vitally to the understanding and being of Church. It is essential that all churches remain open to otherness, as none can claim to be sole possessor of the complete truth. While there are agents other than the church which can call it to attend to its otherness – the prophetic power of the world – of all the institutions that should be alive and attentive to its own otherness, within and without, the church should be the first, as its origin and goal is the one who is 'wholly other'.

(c) In Sacrament

We have within the self-understanding of the church as sacrament the means by which the church can be self-suspicious. The notion of saving suspicion is inherent in the very meaning of sacrament as that which makes present what is other and beyond itself.

This material world in which we live comes from God, but it is easy for us to be so pre-occupied with it that we can become captive to it, residents rather than pilgrims. We can inhabit it in a short-sighted fashion, aware only of its immediacy and immanence, blind to its power to reveal and insensitive to its potential to bring us beyond itself. The sacraments, through the material nature of substances like bread, water, oil, are an invitation and challenge to us to look more deeply at the stuff of the world, to be suspicious of what the senses most immediately receive, and to read and interpret the stuff as of God and from God. 'Human beings see the sacrament, but they must not rest their gaze there on the object. They must transcend the object and see the God communicated in the sacrament.'[57]

At the heart of sacrament is the notion of otherness. Sacrament, with its indicatory and revelatory functions[58] points us to God and at the same time reveals God to us, but is forever other than God. The magical and the superstitious come into play when this quality of otherness is ignored. And church as the sacrament of Christ is other than Christ, despite the church's triumphalist temptations, as we have seen, to identify with him, which would result in idolatry.

Sacrament as suspicion, therefore, because of its quality of otherness, is able to connect us to God, while at the same time safeguarding God as 'wholly other'. Moreover it is in tune with sacrament as eschatological, christological and pastoral.

Eschatological suspicion as a disposition is appropriate because of the 'not yet' quality of the kingdom. If we were not able to be suspicious then the danger would be that the 'already' dimension of the kingdom would eclipse all the other aspects, leading to the false notion of the kingdom being fully present. Suspicion keeps us actively involved with the coming of the kingdom, with the discerning and waiting that such an attitude requires. In regard to the kingdom the concept of sacrament occupies the same space as that of suspicion, having us engage with the 'now' of it through the material realities of the sacramental substances, and yet pointing us beyond through its sign and indicatory nature. Just as with kingdom, there is an 'already – not yet' quality about suspicion which acknowledges there is an 'otherness' (corresponding to the 'not yet') to whatever is (corresponding to the 'already').

Regarding the christological aspect of suspicion, it can be said that Christ carries suspicion into the very centre of the Godhead, and also into the heart of humankind. Something very other is introduced into God when we realise that in the Godhead is the Christ from whom humanity can never be removed. Humanity will forever reside in the Godhead. And secondly, because of his divinity, through the Incarnation Jesus has presented something quite other to us and to our humanity. For the believer there is no such thing as the 'merely' human.

Furthermore, if we look at the whole thrust of Christ's mission and message we see it was toward seeking out 'the other', suspicious always of the tidy and the comfortable. It was the statement spoken by the Incarnation and repeated often in the course of his life: his speaking to the Samaritan woman, eating with tax collectors and dining with sinners. He cautioned us to be suspicious of our own motivations, (Mt 6:1-7) and alerted us to the damage that our internal (unconscious) distortion can cause if we address others without being aware of this: 'take the plank out of your own eye first, and then you will see clearly enough to take out the splinter that is in your brother's eye.' (Lk 6:40-43)

But above all, the paradox of the whole life, death and resurrection of Christ is an ultimate expression of suspicion regarding all that is. A death that is resurrection transforms all that is of life, in how it informs life's meaning. In losing life we can save it, in saving life we can lose it. Living from a perspective where the intangible, such as virtue, is so fundamental, we will inevitably cast a suspicious gaze on everything as it appears to be. Believing in the life, death and resurrection of Christ, we are obliged to carry an inner disposition of suspicion that is saving, enlivening us to the truth that there is a quality of 'otherness' to all that is.

And thirdly, suspicion as we have outlined it, has within it considerable pastoral potential. Initially it might appear to be a negative factor in relationship making. But to the contrary, it can be an act of genuine hope, trust and love.

As hope: generally criticism is about the future and the future of possibilities where the critic believes that the individual's or institution's self-understanding can be greater than it is now, and where a higher moral standard than is lived at present can in fact be reached. When such criticism is self-directed it is about enabling the self toward a better future: '...resistance to ourselves is also hope.'[59]

As trust: because of the risk involved in being suspicious it is often only on the basis of a strong trust that we can engage in such an exercise. Suspicion can in fact be an act of entrusting and giving over, where we make ourselves vulnerable in the way we raise questions about ourselves, and in so doing leaving ourselves open to comment and evaluation.

As love: wanting the very best at any particular time for the other can often be the energy behind suspicion and as such can be an expression of love. To be able to be suspicious of self, and to be open to another's caution about the possibility of moments of blindness or distorted perception is a disposition appropriate to intimacy in relationship, which is a purpose of sacrament. Love requires us no less to challenge ourselves than encourage others, to suspect ourselves than support others.

> A friendship that never includes critique and even, when appropriate, suspicion is a friendship barely removed from the polite and wary communication of strangers... But if that encounter is to prove more than transitory, the difficult ways of friendship need a trust powerful enough to risk itself in critique and suspicion.[60]

Notes

1. Tracy, David: *Plurality and Ambiguity Hermeneutics, Religion and Hope*, San Francisco, Harper and Row, 1987, p 9.
2. Foster, *Modern Ireland 1600-1972*, London, Penguin Press, 1988, p 319.
3. Ricoeur, Paul: *Freud and Philosophy*, New Haven, Yale University Press, 1970, p 32.

4. Tracy, David: op cit supra (n 1). See also Tracy, David: *The Analogical Imagination*, London, S C M, 1981.

5. Tracy: op cit supra (n 1), p 48.

6. Tracy: op cit supra (n 1), p 7.

7. Tracy: op cit supra (n 1), p 22.

8. Tracy: op cit supra (n 1). In this book Tracy deals with the issue of plurality by considering the language we use, (chapter 3 of his book is entitled 'Radical Plurality: The Question of Language') and with the issue of ambiguity being considered in relation to history. In this book I have chosen to focus on the latter, the ambiguous nature of history.

9. Falconer, Alan (ed.): *Reconciling Memories*, Dublin, Columba Press, 1988.

10. Tracy: op cit supra (n 1), p 69, refering to Walter Benjamin.

11. ibid.

12. Tracy: op cit supra (n 1), p 74.

13. Jung, C.G.: *The Undiscovered Self*, London, Routledge and Kegan Paul, 1958. 'We still go on thinking and acting as before, as if we were simplex and not duplex. Accordingly, we imagine ourselves to be inocuous, reasonable and humane. We do not think of distrusting our motives...' p 84.

14. Tracy: op cit supra (n 1), p 77.

15. ibid.

16. Ricoeur: op cit supra (n 3), p 33.

17. Metz, Johann Baptist: The Emergent *Church*, London, S C M, 1981, p 94.

18. Ricoeur: op cit supra (n 3), pp 32-36.

19. Ricoeur: op cit supra (n 3), p 32.

20. Tracy: op cit supra (n 4), pp 346-9.

21. Tracy: op cit supra (n 4), p 349.

22. Ricoeur: op cit supra (n 3), p 34.

23. Because of the negative connotations of the word 'suspicion' I was tempted to replace it with a more positive term. But I think there is a value in maintaining the word. It is accepted in the study of hermeneutics. Moreover its negative character may have a power to arrest attention when it is used in a

positive fashion as saving suspicion, especially when the suspect is oneself rather than someone on the other side.

24. Theunissen, Michael: *The Other Studies in the Social Ontology of Husserl, Heidegger, Sartre and Buber*, Massachusetts, Massachusetts Institute of Technology, 1984. 'Few issues have exercised as powerful a hold over the thought of this century as that of 'the Other'... The question of the Other cannot be separated from the most primordial questions raised by modern thought.' p 1. See also Levinas, Emmanuel: *Totality and Infinity*, Dortrecht, Nijhoff Publication, 1980.

25. Schussler Fiorenza, Elizabeth: 'The Politics of Otherness: Biblical Interpretation as a Critical Praxis for Liberation.' Ellis, Marc and Maduro, Otto (eds.): *The Future of Liberation Theology*, New York, Orbis, 1989, pp 311-326. See also Barth, Karl: *The Epistle to the Romans*, London, Oxford University Press, 1933, pp 42,49.

26. Otto, Rudolf: *The Idea of the Holy*, London, Oxford University Press, 1923

27. Otto: op cit supra (n 26), p 5.

28. Otto: op cit supra (n 26), p 25.

29. Otto: op cit supra (n 26), p 31.

30. Jung: op cit supra (n 13), p 83.

31. Tracy: op cit supra (n 1), p 78.

32. Tracy: op cit supra (n 1), p 79.

33. Jung: op cit supra (n 13), p 83.

34. Tracy: op cit supra (n 1), p 73.

35. Ricoeur: op cit supra (n 3), p 33.

36. Tracy: op cit supra (n 1), p 69.

37. Tracy: op cit supra (n 1), p 15.

38. ibid.

39. Tracy: op cit supra (n 4), p 451.

40. Jung: op cit supra (n 13), p 103.

41. Jung: op cit supra (n 13), p 102.

42. Baum, Gregory: *Religion and Alienation*, New York, Paulist Press, 1975, p 62. See also Houtepen, Anton: *People of God: A*

Plea for the Church, London, S C M, 1984. 'The paradigm of prophet keeps the church from becoming fossilized, because prophecy is again and again the renewing force which interprets the tradition afresh in new situations.' p 158.

43. Wilson, Robert: 'Early Israelite Prophecy.' Mays, James Luther and Achtemeier, Paul (eds.): *Interpreting the Prophets*, Philadelphia, Fortress Press, 1987, pp 1-14, p 7.

44. Power,John: *Set My Exiles Free*, Dublin, Gill and Son, 1967, p 112.

45. Berger, Peter: *The Sacred Canopy*, New York, Doubleday, 1969, p 100.

46. Mc Donagh, Enda: *Demands of Simple Justice*, Dublin, Gill and Macmillan, 1980 pp 41-2.

47. de Gruchy, John: *Theology and Ministry in Context and Crisis*, London, Collins, 1987, p 76.

48. O'Leary, Joseph: 'Religion, Ireland: in Mutation.' *Across the Frontier*, Kearney, Richard (ed.) Dublin, Wolfhound Press, 1988, pp 231-240. 'What is peculiarly dangerous in the case of Catholicism is the creed that the Church, since it is not a human institution at all but a divine one, can do no wrong. The Catholic Church has long regarded certain figures and texts as above suspicion, much as doctrinaire Marxists used to hallow Marx or Lenin. The lesson we are having to learn now is that even the pages of the New Testament, and much more so those of Saints Athanasius, Augustine, Bernard of Clairvaux and Thomas Aquinas have to be read with suspicion.' pp 238-9.

49. Jung: op cit supra (n 13), p 102.

50. Mc Donagh: *Doing the Truth*, Dublin, Gill and Macmillan, 1979, p 195.

51. Abbott, Walter (gen.ed.): *The Documents of Vatican II*, New York, Guild Press, 1966. *Unitatis Redintegratio*, p 350, par 6.

52. Abbott: op cit supra (n 51), *Lumen Gentium*. '...that moved by the Holy Spirit she (the Church) may never cease to purify herself...' p 26, par 9.

53. Abbott: op cit supra (n 51), *Unitatis Redintegratio*, p 350, par 6.

54. Abbott: op cit supra (n 51), *Lumen Gentium*, p 23, par 8.
55. ibid.
56. Abbott: op cit supra (n 51), *Unitatis Redintegratio*, p 346, par 3.
57. Boff: *Sacraments of Life and Life of the Sacraments*, Washington, Pastoral Press, 1987, p 32.
58. Boff: op cit supra (n 57), p 31.
59. Tracy: op cit supra (n 1), p 72.
60. Tracy: op cit supra (n 1), p 112.

CHAPTER 4

Saving Suspicion and the Church

1. THE CURRENT RESPONSE

How open does the church, in the context of its sacramental ecclesiology, appear to be to this notion of saving suspicion that I have been developing? The question can be posed in relation to very different situations, and Joseph O'Leary is forthright in what he has to say about the situation in Ireland: 'It (the Irish Catholic Church) fears the pain of this probing, and prefers to hold on to its surface equilibrium rather than embark on a process so upsetting.'[1] I surmise that this assessment could apply to denominations other than the Roman Catholic Church, and that is for others to assess. Here I wish to address the local situation and stay with the context that I outlined in the introduction, with the focus on the Roman Catholic Church.

What evidence of openness to saving suspicion is there in the response of the bishops to the northern violence? How prepared are they to be self-questioning, self-critical, self-suspicious in this regard? With condemnation of others having such a high profile in statements from the bishops, it would not be surprising to find that critical self-reflection does not figure frequently in their output. They appear to see it as their primary duty to stress to their own community the evil of violence and the need for peace, forgiveness and reconciliation.[2] It is very much in the mode of the institutional church to speak from a position of authority to those 'under' its care; overall that appears to be the self-understanding of the Irish church as expressed through the bishops' statements. This leaves little room for the dialogical character of sacrament that we have seen in chapter 1.

But now and again there would appear to be an openness on the part of the bishops to be self-critical, in terms of looking at the church's part in the violence. Before coming to Down and Connor Bishop Cahal Daly said:

> If the motives of politicians in blaming the Churches can be questioned, however, it is equally incumbent on us church-men to question the motives which lead us to deny the charge and to refuse blame and responsibility... Yet I am deeply convinced that the Churches have a certain blame for the genesis of the situation and a real responsibility in regard to it...[3]

He then goes on to talk quite explicitly about the place and value of criticism:

> Criticisms made openly in the presence of the criticised are less offensive and less harmful than criticisms made *in absentia* before an audience of 'one's own kind.' Even painful criticism can be healing if spoken honestly and openly in love.[4]

When preaching in Belfast in May 1986 he said:

> Reconciliation will mean acknowledging our own sins, be-ing ready to forgive wrongs done against us and recognising that we have all, as individuals and institutions, things to repent of...[5]

And he is on record as calling for what I have named suspicion:

> There should be no excusation (sic!) for anyone who uses the tragic Northern situation to advance some other cause or in-terest of his own, whether it be political or theological. Here again, however, one must confess that it is easier to call for utter honesty from others than to detect and eliminate con-cealed dishonesty in oneself. One can only try.[6]

Bishop Edward Daly cautions us a number of times on the need for self-examination:

We find it easy to blame other people for the ills of the world and our own problems. We are less inclined to examine the contribution that we ourselves have made to those problems.[7]

And again:

....we must constantly examine our own consciences. [8]

While these sentiments have been expressed, there does not appear to be any sustained follow-through on these insights. They signal a desire to consider suspicion regarding the church's involvement, but have not been acted on. There has been nothing from the bishops that would give clear indication of what they feel the church has been responsible for in the present violence, nor any substantial account of what they think has been the church's contribution to the troubles over the years.[9] So, while the bishops have acknowledged the shadow of the church in principle, they have been unable or unwilling to spell this out, and so have avoided meeting head on the practical implications of the human character, and thus the full sacramentality, of the church.

One could ask, in the spirit of suspicion, why the question of the church's responsibility has not been taken up by the bishops. Is it simply that it is too difficult to sustain a self-critical, sacramental perspective in the midst of daily violence and frequent killing? Could it be that the practice of suspicion, even saving suspicion, cannot be maintained by any church in a situation where church membership and community identity are so closely bound up together? Or could it be that it is felt that the mere voicing of the need for suspicion suffices, and perhaps any follow through would risk giving away too much to the other side? If this were the situation, then, consciously or unconsciously, such a church would be less than the sacrament it claims to be. A truly sacramental church could only be inclusive in its embrace, and courageous in its openness to what is other, and in being so it would inevitably contribute to easing the 'fear, suspicion, ignorance and prejudice, which can rightly be termed sectarian.'[10] A church other than this would be open to the accusation of being sectarian.[11]

71

Bishop Cahal Daly shows himself very understanding of suspicion, ('...beware of man's limitless faculty for self-deception.')[12] concerning the motivations, conscious and unconscious, that people may have when they are being critical of others. He uses these insights to warn against the 'glow of moral satisfaction to be procured by public confession of the guilt of one's own Church,'[13] and against the 'pharisaism of the publican.'[14] While there is wisdom in such caution, the church must open itself to the same suspicious gaze, must equally 'beware of man's limitless faculty for self-deception' regarding its own avoidance of any substantial critical self-questioning in relation to the recent northern violence. Such avoidance smacks of the reluctance at Vatican II of the church to own its share in the sinfulness of the world. What might emerge if such self-questioning were to happen?

2. THE SUSPICIOUS RESPONSE

If the Roman Catholic Church were to become more suspicious of itself, more self-critical, it would be totally congruent with its self-understanding as sacrament. Inviting the Roman Catholic Church to be self-suspicious through sacrament is asking it to address itself from within the heart of its own tradition, as we have seen in chapter 3 the prophets did to Israel. Moreover, this approach would permit us to take into account the particular context. In the spirit of local or contextual theology[15] it would bring the traditional concepts inherent in sacrament into contact with the local culture and thereby enrich these concepts. 'As in all good theology, so here too the way which leads to knowledge runs from the specific to the universal, and not vice versa.' [16]

And so to the particular context of Northern Ireland – how might such an understanding of sacrament influence the Roman Catholic Church in Northern Ireland as we have seen it reflected in the words of its bishops? In responding to that question I intend to take up again the three aspects of the church as sacrament that I have considered in chapters 1 and 2 – firstly the christological, then the pastoral and thirdly the eschatological – and bring them into dialogue with what is revealed through saving suspicion in the context of Northern Ireland.

(a) 'Making-Possibilities-Possible'[17]

Vatican II was at pains to stress the christological nature of the church each time it described it as sacrament.[18] One of the purposes of this approach is to underline the fact that the church is not self-sufficient. It appears that the church needs to be reminded of such a truth in order to guard against the tendency to see itself primarily in terms of being 'the spotless spouse,'[19] and 'the edifice of God.'[20] We have seen that there is a temptation for the Roman Catholic Church to ignore, in a triumphalist way, the human dimension of the church, and to attempt to divinise itself beyond the Godhead which incorporates the humanity of Christ. A truly sacramental church, embracing the humanity of Christ, would be alert to such triumphalist tendencies of ignoring the distinction between the church and the divine.

In relation to Northern Ireland, it could be claimed that the triumphalist face of the Roman Catholic Church is shown in the way that it has become so identified with condemnations, 'in language stressing his (the person condemned) total exclusion from the society of the speaker.'[21] I am not saying that a church open to being suspicious about itself would thereby need to refrain from condemnation. But I believe that a church, alive to its christological character and aware of its weakness and failure, would seriously question both the purpose and content of the condemnations it issues, would have more options other than condemnation, and when condemning, would be able to do so with real credibility and effect.

It is so easy and such a danger for the church of whatever denomination to appear to be self-righteous when it condemns – 'we are right and you are wrong!' – and there is the trap not only of scapegoating but also of deluding ourselves into thinking that we are dealing with violence by condemning it. Suspicion regarding condemnation, especially frequent condemnation, could lead us to consider, among other things, the dynamic of projection, described in chapter 3 above. As I have already outlined, this dynamic is the defence mechanism whereby we attribute to others, unconsciously, thoughts and feelings which belong to ourselves but which are not accepted as such, and thus others are blamed for what we are unable to face up to in ourselves. It is not being suggested that such is the sole motivation for the church's condemnation of the people of violence. The church sees evil in the violence and is duty bound to condemn it. But questions arise about condemnation which is always directed outside ourselves to others, and about the possible influence of the dynamic of projection in such behaviour. If the Roman Catholic Church were more open to its own failures, its own 'shadows,'[22] and through suspicion were alive to its possible collusion in sectarianism,[23] in seeking and maintaining its own power while claiming to serve,[24] in aligning itself with the nationalist perspective,[25] then the tone and maybe the content of the condemnations would be different. They would issue from a body alive to its own wrongdoing, and coloured by a sense of common failure, with much less chance of being tainted by self-righteousness. How different might have been the statement of November 9, 1987 that I referred to in the introduction, if it had engaged with these realities? And this has as much relevance for the priest in his homily as for the bishop in his statement, where particular condemnation cannot lose sight of communal culpability. Could it be envisaged that the church might have to ask the paramilitaries for forgiveness for the ways it has sent ambiguous messages to them, if not at the present then in the recent past?

And what else might be possible, not replacing condemnation but supplementing it? We have already seen Bishop Cahal Daly on a number of occasions appealing to the people of violence in an invitatory fashion,[26] which is in tune with the dialogical character of sacrament. Such appeals, coming from an awareness of vulnerability, bespeak a very different church than does the ritual denunciation and predictable condemnation. And a church alive to its own shadow would be open to explore, not just non-violent alternatives, but ways, e.g. through liturgy, of giving expression to genuine hurt, anger and frustration, and also to its own culpability and failure regarding its response to the violence. The church in Northern Ireland today, which sees itself as sacrament, is challenged to create liturgy and ritual which can give expression to outrage and anger, a liturgy that celebrates the shadow, and calls the church to confess its own neglect and failure.

Since 1968, and for centuries back, each community in the North could recite its own litany of outrages. And while there may be argument about different incidents, disagreement about the how and why of various tragedies, there probably is a common response to the outrages themselves, an immediate and very primitive sense of anger. There are many reasons why the community might try to suppress or ignore this anger. But the human condition requires that such experiences be wrestled with, even at the risk of sustaining a Jacob-like limp. And the pastoral nature of the church requires that, as sacrament and as be-coming, it not only be open to such brokenness, but would actively embrace it in order that the healing power of God could become present to it. This is an expression of sacrament, of Moltmann's 'making-possibilities possible'[27] because such liturgy 'keeps the future open to all open systems, and opens the future anew,'[28] that being the very purpose of sacrament.

Surely the Judaeo-Christian story has a richness of resources at its disposal to help the community to and through this wrestling in the context of liturgy: the God of fury and vengeance, the Christ, terrified and in desolation on the cross, yet praying for forgiveness for those who crucified him. In the end the challenge of Christ is to forgive. But the challenge is debased if we imagine that such a response can be automatic. For many forgiveness is a journey, a process, involving the courage to acknowledge the dark angers and resentments. A church reluctant to claim its own darkness, its otherness, can be of little use to people on such a journey.

Forgiveness can be spoken about only by those who have made themselves vulnerable, and know of their own failings. Going out in forgiveness to others must be accompanied by the journey inwards, going in on ourselves in confession and repentance. This is a most difficult journey, and above all for a church which is ambiguous about owning fully its human condition. The church is challenged to confess its collusion in matters such as promoting sectarianism and protecting its own power. It is challenged to own up to its contribution to the deadly mix of nationalism and church affiliation, to confess its tribal sins,[29] because 'to acknowledge the tragedy and our own complicity in it is essential to the hope embodied in Christian conversion.'[30]

(b) 'Similarity-in-Difference'[31]

As the fully pastoral church is christologically orientated much of what I have just said above also speaks to the pastoral context. (I have earlier referred to this over-lap of the christological with the pastoral.) We have seen that the Roman Catholic Church in Northern Ireland is strongly pastoral in its presence to the brokenness of its own community. And we have identified a risk in this type of presence in that it can trap the clergy into the role of being tribal chaplains, and so actually hinder the pastoral dimension of the church as sacrament. There are very strong forces, historical and social, pressurising the clergy into such a role, and collusion on their part keeping them there. I believe that this was the predicament I was struggling with, without being able to name it as possible collusion with tribal chaplaincy, when Michael, whom I spoke of in the introduction, approached me with the request about the use of the parish hall for his republican band. Any perspective, therefore, which could enable the clergy and people, in whatever small way, to move beyond this mutual restriction would have a positive contribution to make in freeing the church toward being more fully sacramental in its pastoral presence.

Suspicion, as we have seen, can open us up to the other existing within, the other that we prefer not to admit to or face, because of how it can complicate the more simple and single-stranded image we have of ourselves. Acknowledging the darker side of itself by the church need not necessarily be a step on the road to fragmentation, but, where a relatively adequate sense of identity is present, it can enable the church to become less defensive and to develop new strength and stability in identity.[32]

The church in Ireland, therefore, has much to gain and much to offer by adopting a stance of critical questioning, or suspicion, towards itself. It exists in a society where there is great confusion regarding self-identity: '...the basic fear on both sides is that of absorption by the other and so permanent loss of identity.'[33] As a result there are different groups abusing and attacking other groups in an effort to sustain and build up their own identity over against the other, and at the expense of the other. The other is primarily and fundamentally experienced as threat. It is in such a setting that tribal chaplaincy flourishes, with each group remaining within its own territory, turned in on itself. Is it not possible that the Irish Catholic Church, relying on the security of its own identity out of it being a world-wide and age old institution, could trust itself enough to embrace otherness without fearing any diminishment in identity? By being open to embrace otherness initially in itself through suspicion, it could have the strength to drop its guard and gain credibility for openness to otherness in the community at large. Such a church would be not just a church for others[34] but a church of others, where difference would not be seen as threat or viewed with suspicion. This perspective has very practical implications, for example in relation to the very sensitive and complex debate about integrated education.

Suspicion of self on the part of the church, then, could facilitate breaking through the suspicion of each other by the communities. Thus suspicion itself would indeed be saving. When otherness is recognised we can then acknowledge the other as possible, and 'when possibility enters, some similarity-in-difference cannot be far behind.'[35] And so the church, by suspecting itself, far from doing damage, could begin to show the community the way toward living together. In so doing it would give expression to its sacramental nature in a pastoral way. It would be sacrament for and to the world, both witnessing to and pastorally creating genuine community, in itself and in the world of Northern Ireland, and through that in the wider world, enabling us to envisage 'possibilities we have never dared to dream.'[36]

(c) 'Bringer of Plurabilities' [37]

The purpose of the church is to preach, promote and, in part, realise the kingdom, 'which is not just a spiritual reality confined to the next life, but a call to a new concrete set of relations in this world, a set of relations that must include all men and women who are Christ's brothers and sisters (Mt 25).'[38]. The emphasis here is on all men and women. A church taking kingdom seriously and believing itself to be sign and sacrament 'of the unity of all mankind'[39] and womankind, would never accomodate to a system of tribal chaplaincy and would see such an arrangement as a contradiction of its very nature and purpose. Rather its basis would be: "…no more distinctions between Jew and Greek, slave and free, male and female, but all of you are one in Christ Jesus.' (Gal 3:28) Such a church would indeed be catholic, concerned with 'the whole of society, not just the part of it with which it is by reason of history, culture, etc. more closely associated – for God is concerned with all.'[40]

It could be said that belief in kingdom gives us not just the right but the duty to suspect all that is, in the light of whether it promotes the kingdom. Since our call is to become kingdom dwellers, all commitments that we make during our lives are relative, relative to the kingdom. Commitment to country, for instance, in the shape of nationalism, has great potential for enrichment, offering a sense of identity through a shared culture and language. But when such a commitment stirs us to think of others in terms of 'outsiders,' or 'the traditional enemy' is there not the beginnings of 'cultural isolationism or xenophobia'?[41] Such a perspective not only does nothing to promote the health of the national culture, but is laying claim to some absolute ownership that does not reflect the truth that we are a pilgrim people on the way to the kingdom.

It is now generally accepted among commentators and historians that the Irish churches have allowed themselves to be aligned to particular ideologies, e.g. Catholics with nationalism.[42] This may have been done for a variety of reasons, some of which may have been understandable at a particular time, e.g. a desire to help the oppressed or to provide a sense of belonging and identity. But it must be acknowledged that such alignment has compromised, and to an extent continues to compromise, the church's identity as a sacrament of the kingdom; hence the danger of being seen to collude with any attempt at paramilitary display at funerals, and the need for a clear understanding of the place of a church servive on such occasions. Because of the historical alignment, the church must take great care to act in a way that is trans-cultural and trans-national and be a church that emphasises that 'the Kingdom is not just for Israel but for many 'who will come from East and West"(Mt 8:11).[43]

Bishop Cahal Daly has spoken of the danger of 'the relativising of religion... or the replacement of the true God by political and secular idols.'[44] He went on to say that there are Catholics and Protestants guilty of this, who regard their political allegiance as absolute, and 'subsitute what is not God for God. It is a form of idolatry.'[45] The truth of this would be all the clearer and all the more convincing if, through being suspicious of itself, the church were able to acknowledge that it has colluded in this process by aligning itself with nationalism, and secondly, that the church itself is relative, relative to the kingdom, and thus is also in danger of being guilty of idolatry.

> From the biblical point of view, the Church itself could become an idol ... The Church is tempted by idolatry when

it wants to multiply the absolutes and regard its teaching and its hierarchy as the ultimate norms for judging all forms of Christian life and faith.[46]

This is not to imply that the church cannot at times be forthright in its teaching and its hierarchy outspoken in its message. But it seems that a church, open to suspect itself and aware of its own temptation and guilt, would know of itself as quite other than kingdom, and thus would address others from a position of being fellow traveller, rather than as one who too often gives the impression of looking back from the promised land.

In summary, then, by incorporating saving suspicion into the church's self-understanding as sacrament, we would have a church that would consider it being most true to its tradition in being open to on-going self-questioning and renewal. It would be a dynamic church, believing in itself as be-coming, and committed to the process of ecclesiogenesis. Welcoming the other as fellow traveller, dialogue rather than distance would mark its disposition. As a result it would be very alert to the danger and damage of triumphalism. When appropriate, it could respond to situations by condemnation, but that would be only one of a range of responses which would be geared more to support and conversion than to denunciation, to making possibilities possible than to alerting consciences to evil. Such a church could give leadership in creating community through trusting itself to cross boundaries within and without in truly catholic fashion, and so encouraging others to follow its example. It would struggle against being trapped in the web of traditional alignments, and would find its inspiration more from Joyce's 'bringer of plurabilities'[47] than from the counter-kingdom tribal chaplain.

Notes

1. O'Leary, Joseph: 'Religion, Ireland: in Mutation'. Kearney, Richard (ed.): *Across the Frontiers*, Dublin, Wolfhound Press, 1988, pp 231-240, p 240.

2. Bishop Cahal Daly's address to Dublin University Historical Society, 1975: 'They (the clergy and the hierarchy of the church) should, on the basis of the Gospel itself, expose and denounce false judgements, the suspicions, the culpable ignorance and, sometimes, the still more culpable cupidity and dishonesty, which lead to sectarian and racial prejudice.' See also Bishop Cahal Daly's address at Heythrop College, London, 24 November, 1984: 'As a churchman, I must and with God's help I shall, in common with my fellow bishops and with all my clergy, go on proclaiming Christian moral teaching about murder and violence, and go on unremittingly proclaiming the Christian Gospel of love, forgiveness and peace.'

3. Daly, Cahal: 'Northern Tragedy: Challenge to the Churches'. Daly, Cahal: *Peace, the Work of Justice*, Dublin, Veritas, 1979, pp 1-35, pp 3,4.

4. Daly: op cit supra (n 3), p 5.

5. Bishop Cahal Daly's homily at the Ecumenical Service for Pentecost, in St Malachy's Church, Belfast, 18 May, 1986.

6. Daly: *Peace, the Work of Justice* , op cit supra (n 3), p 2.

7. Bishop Edward Daly's address to St Columb's College Past Pupils Union, 19 November, 1982.

8. Bishop Edward Daly's address to St Columb's College Past Pupils Union, 18 October, 1985.

9. Working Party of Irish Council of Churches and Roman Catholic Church Joint Group on Social Questions, *Violence in Ireland, a Report to the Churches*, Belfast, Christian Journals, Dublin, Veritas, 1976. 'All organisations and bodies, not excluding the Churches themselves and certainly including those orders with religious or quasi-religious conditions of membership, must ask themselves fearlessly to what extent their actions and stances, no matter what their theological

foundation, may contribute to the separation which can produce the terrible results that have occurred in recent years. The Churches have not adequately faced up to the consequences of this religious segregation.' p 71 This indicates awareness of the fact of the church's contribution, but there is little evidence of any movement on the strength of this awareness.

10. *Violence in Ireland: A Report to the Churches*, op cit supra (n 9), p 72.

11. Connolly, Peter: 'The Church in Ireland since Vatican II.' *The Furrow*, Vol 30, No 12, 1979, pp 755-766. 'As churchmen reflect on the recent history of Christianity in Ireland they must at some point face the fact of their own contribution to the present conflict in the North: the sectarianism they have allowed to flourish in the past or sometimes covertly encouraged.' p 765

12. Daly: *Peace, the Work of Justice* , op cit supra (n 3), p 6.

13. ibid.

14. ibid.

15. Schreiter, Robert: *Constructing Local Theologies*, London, SCM, 1985.

16. Witvliet, Theo: *A Place in the Sun, Liberation Theology in the Third World*, London, S C M, 1985, Preface viii.

17. Moltmann: *God in Creation* , London, S C M, 1985, p 182.

18. Abbott, Walter (gen. ed.): *The Documents of Vatican II*, New York, Guild Press, 1966. *Lumen Gentium*, p 15, par 1; p 79, par 48. *Sacrosanctum Concilium*, p 140, par 5.

19. Abbott: op cit supra (n 18), *Lumen Gentium*, p 19. par 6.

20. ibid.

21. Bishop Cahal Daly in an interview with James Downey, *Irish Times*, 16 August, 1976.

22. Schillebeeckx, Edward: *Mission of the Church*, London, Sheed and Ward, 1973, p 7.

23. Connolly: op cit supra (n 11), p 765.

24. Mc Donagh: *The Demands of Simple Justice*, Dublin, Gill and Macmillan, 1980, p 43.

25. Mc Donagh, Enda: 'A Church for the World'. Falconer, Alan; Mc Donagh, Enda; Mac Réamoinn, Seán; (eds.), *Freedom to Hope?* Dublin, Columba Press, 1985, pp 82-93, pp 91-2.
26. Bishop Cahal Daly's homily at the funeral of Miss Mary Travers, 11 April, 1984. See also Bishop Cahal Daly's address at a service in St. Anne's Cathedral, 16 March, 1987.
27. Moltmann: op cit supra (n 17), p 182.
28. Moltmann: op cit supra (n 17), pp 182-3.
29. A Repentance Service of this nature, led by Rev Neal Carlin and Rev Alan Harper, took place on Good Friday, 1985, in the Guildhall Square in Derry.
30. Mc Donagh: op cit supra (n 25), p 91.
31. Tracy: *Plurality and Ambiguity*, San Francisco, Harper and Row, 1987, p 20.
32. Tracy: *Analogical Imagination*, London, S C M, 1981. 'If I, as a Catholic Christian, have really faced the critique of the Catholic understanding of love as caritas by Protestant theologians, if I have actually experienced, in critical conversation, the force of the critiques of suspicion upon all Christian understandings of love as compassion, agape or caritas in Freud, Marx and Nietzsche, then I should have exited from those conversations transformed. I may, in fact I do find that the Catholic caritas understanding of Christian love remains the focussed ideal of my life. Yet I also know that my earlier willingness to try to understand alternative options for understanding love and to try to appropriate their critiques of certain realities in my own focal meaning have subtly transformed, purified and enriched my rootedness in my own caritas tradition.' p 452.
33. McDonagh, Enda: *Violence and Political Change*, London, Catholic Institute for International Relations, 1978, p 18. See also Falconer, 'Remembering'. *Studies*, Vol 78, No 310, 1989, pp 169-176. 'The identity of each community has been shaped by the actions, attitudes and declarations of other communities... Since each community is associated with a different ecclesiastical tradition, it is important to emphasise

that the different Churches have also emphasised their identity in opposition to other Churches.' p 171. See also Trew, Karen: 'A Sense of National Identity – Fact or Artefact?' *Irish Journal of Psychology*, Vol 6, No 1. Autumn 1983, pp 28-36.

34. Western European Working Group and North American Working Group of the Department on Studies in Evangelism: *The Church For Others*, London, W.C.C., 1968.

35. Tracy: op cit supra (n 31), p 20.

36. Tracy: op cit supra (n 31), p 79.

37. Quoted by Kearney, Richard: 'Myth and the Critique of Tradition.' Falconer, Alan (ed.): *Reconciling Memories*, Dublin, Columba Press, 1988, pp 8-24, p 20.

38. 'Breaking down the Enmity'. 2.4, Inter-Church Group on Faith and Politics: *Choose Life*, Inter-Church Group on Faith and Politics, Belfast, 1987.

39. Abbott: op cit supra (n 18), *Lumen Gentium*, p 15, par 1.

40. Inter-Church Group on Faith and Politics: op cit supra (n 38), 3.3

41. Mc Donagh, *Gift and Call*, Dublin, Gill and Macmillan, 1979, p 133.

42. Mc Donagh, Enda: 'Dying for the Cause: An Irish Perspective on Martyrdom'. Mc Donagh, Enda: *Between Chaos and New Creation*, Dublin, Gill and Macmillan, 1986, pp 123-132. 'It is from the inevitable convergence of these two struggles for Catholic Emancipation and political independence that the present-day intertwining of Catholicism and Nationalism stems.' p 127.
See also O'Brien, C C: 'Religion and Nationalism'. Lynch, Patrick; Meenan, James; (eds.): *Essays in Memory of Alexis Fitzgerald*, Dublin, The Incorporated Law Society of Ireland, 1987, pp 89-104. 'At a deep level there is, I believe, felt to be an identity between Irish Catholicism and Irish nationality, though this is almost never formally asserted, and is even officially denied.' p 90.
See also Lyons, F S L: *Culture and Anarchy in Ireland 1890-1939*, London, Oxford University Press, 1979. 'The drift

towards the Gaelic, Catholic concept of nationality seems
unmistakable.' p 169.
See also Villa-Vicencio, Charles: 'Theology in the service of
the State: the Steyn and Eloff Commissions'. Villa-Vicencio,
Charles and De Gruchy, John (eds.), *South African Essays in
Honour of Beyers Naude*, Michigan, Eerdmans, 1985, 112-125.
In this essay Villa-Vicencio writes of 'theologised national-
ism,' or 'patriotic theology.' p 113.

43. Inter-Church Group on Faith and Politics: op cit supra (n
38), 2.3.
44. Daly, Cahal: 'Northern Ireland: Risk and Opportunity for
the Churches'. Address given at a Conference on the Role of
the Churches in British-Irish Relationships, in Dublin, 26
November, 1985.
45. ibid.
46. Baum, Gregory: *Religion and Alienation*, New York, Paulist
Press, 1975, p 64.
47. Quoted by Kearney, Richard: 'Myth and the Critique of
Tradition'. op cit supra (n 37), p 20.

Bibliography

Abbott, Walter S.J. (ed.): *The Documents of Vatican II*,
New York, The American Press, 1966.

Baum, Gregory: *Religion and Alienation*,
New York, Paulist Press, 1975.

Berger, Peter: *The Sacred Canopy*,
New York, Doubleday and Co. Inc., 1969.

Best, Thomas (ed.): *Faith and Renewal, Reports and
Documents of the Commission on Faith and Order,
Stavanger, 1985, Norway*, Faith and Order Paper
No. 131, Geneva, W.C.C., 1986.

Boff, Leonardo: *Ecclesio-genesis*,
London, Collins, 1986.
Sacraments of Life and Life of the Sacraments,
Washington, Pastoral Press, 1987.
Trinity and Society,
London, Burns and Oates, 1988.

Bonino, Jose Miguez: *Doing Theology in a Revolutionary Situation*,
Philadelphia, Fortress Press, 1975.

Boyd, Robin: *Ireland, Christianity Discredited or Pilgrim's Progress?*,
Geneva, W.C.C., 1988.

Brueggemann, Walter: *The Prophetic Imagination*,
Philadelphia, Fortress Press, 1978.

Connolly, Peter: 'The Church in Ireland since Vatican II'.
The Furrow, Vol 30, No 12, 1979, pp 755-766.

Daly, Cahal B.: *Peace, the Work of Justice*,
Dublin, Veritas, 1979.

Darby, John: *Conflict in Northern Ireland*,
Dublin, Gill and Macmillan, 1976.
(ed.): *Northern Ireland The Background to the Conflict*,
Belfast, Appletree Press, 1983.

Dulles, Avery S.J.: *Models of the Church*,
    Dublin, Gill and Macmillan, 1976.
    A Church to Believe In,
    New York, Crossroads, 1982.
    The Catholicity of the Church,
    Oxford, Clarendon Press, 1985.
Ellis, Marc and Maduro, Otto (eds.):
    The Future of Liberation Theology,
    New York, Orbis Books, 1989.
Falconer, Alan, Mc Donagh, Enda and MacRéamoinn, Seán (eds.)
    Freedom to Hope?
    Dublin, Columba Press, 1985.
Falconer,Alan (ed.): *Reconciling Memories*,
    Dublin, Columba Press, 1988.
    'Remembering'. *Studies*, Vol 78, No 310, 1989, pp 169-176.
    'The Churches: Pilgrims or Residents?' *Doctrine and Life*,
    Vol 40, 1990, pp 4-10.
Foster, Roy: *Modern Ireland 1600-1972*,
    London, Penguin Press, 1988.
Gallagher, Eric & Worrall, Stanley: *Christians in Ulster 1968-1980*,
    London, Oxford University Press, 1982.
de Gruchy, John W: *Theology and Ministry in Context and Crisis*,
    London, Collins, 1987.
Hanna, Eamon (ed.): *Reconciliation in Northern Ireland* ,
    Dublin, Social Study Conference Publications, 1987.
Hickey, John: *Religion and The Northern Ireland Problem*,
    Dublin, Gill and Macmillan, 1984.
Houtepen, Anton: *People of God A Plea for the Church*,
    London, S C M, 1984.
    'Towards an Ecumenical Vision of the Church'.
    One in Christ, Vol 25, No 3, 1989, pp 217-237.
Inter-Church Group on Faith and Politics: *Choose Life*
    Christian Responses to the Northern Ireland Conflict,
    Inter-Church Group on Faith and Politics, Belfast, 1986.
Irish Bishops: *Justice, Love and Peace: Pastoral Letters of the Irish
    Bishops 1969-1979*, Dublin, Veritas, 1979.

Jung, Carl C: *The Undiscovered Self*,
    London, Routledge and Kegan Paul Ltd., 1958.
Kairos Theologians: *Kairos Document Challenge to the Church*,
    London, Catholic Institute for International Relations and
    British Council of Churches, 1985.
Kasper, Walter: *Theology and Church*,
    London, S C M, 1989.
Kearney, Richard (ed.): *Across the Frontiers*,
    Dublin, Wolfhound Press, 1988.
Kness, Robert: *The Church: Communion, Sacrament, Communication*,
    New York, Paulist Press, 1985.
Limouris, Gennadios (ed.): *Church, Kingdom, World: The Church as*
    Mystery and Prophetic Sign,
    Faith and Order Paper No.130, Geneva, W.C.C., 1986.
de Lubac, Henri: *Catholicism A Study of Dogma in Relation to the*
    Corporate Destiny of Mankind,
    London, Burns and Oates, 1950.
Lynch, Patrick and Meenan, James (eds.):
    Essays in Memory of Alexis Fitzgerald,
    Dublin, The Incorporated Law Society of Ireland, 1987.
Lyons, F S L: *Culture and Anarchy in Ireland 1890-1939*,
    London, Oxford University Press, 1979.
Mays,James Luther and Achtemeier Paul J (eds.):
    Interpreting the Prophets,
    Philadelphia, Fortress Press, 1987.
Metz, Johann Baptist: *Theology of the World*,
    London, Herder and Herder, 1969.
    The Emergent Church, London, S C M, 1981.
Minear, Paul: *Images of the Church in the New Testament*,
    Philadelphia, The Westminster Press, 1960.
Moltmann, Jurgen: *The Crucified God*,
    London, S C M, 1974.
    The Trinity and the Kingdom of God,
    London, S C M, 1981.
    God in Creation,
    London, S C M, 1985.

Mc Afee Brown, Robert :*Theology in a New Key*,
 Philadelphia, Westminster Press, 1978.
Mc Brien, Richard P: *Do We Need the Church?*,
 London, Collins, 1969.
Mc Donagh, Enda: *Gift and Call*,
 Dublin, Gill and Macmillan, 1979.
 Violence and Political Change,
 London, Catholic Institute for International Relations, 1978.
 The Demands of Simple Justice,
 Dublin, Gill and Macmillan, 1980.
 Between Chaos and New Creation, Doing Theology at the Fringe,
 Dublin, Gill and Macmillan, 1986.
Mc Donagh, Enda (ed.): *Irish Challenges to Theology: Papers of the Irish Theological Association Conference 1984*,
 Dublin, Dominican Publications, 1986.
Mac Donagh, Oliver: *States of Mind A Study of Anglo-Irish Conflict 1780-1980*,
 London, George Allen and Unwin Ltd., 1983.
O'Brien, C C: *States of Ireland*,
 London, Hutchinson, 1972.
O'Malley, Padraig: *The Uncivil Wars*,
 Belfast, Blackstaff Press, 1983.
Otto, Rudolf: *The Idea of the Holy*,
 London, Oxford University Press, 1923.
Pannenberg, Wolfhart: *Basic Questions in Theology Vol.2*,
 London, S C M, 1971.
Power, John: *Set My Exiles Free*,
 Dublin, Gill and Son, 1967.
Rahner, Karl: *The Church and the Sacraments*,
 London, Burns and Oates, 1963.
 Theological Investigations Vol.6,
 Baltimore, Helicon, 1969.
Rea, Desmond (ed.): *Political Co-operation in Divided Societies, A Series of Papers Relevant to the Conflict in Northern Ireland*,
 Dublin, Gill and Macmillan, 1982.

Ricoeur, Paul: *Freud and Philosophy*,
    New Haven, Yale University Press, 1970.
Schillebeeckx, Edward O P: *Christ the Sacrament*,
    London, Sheed and Ward, 1963.
    The Mission of the Church,
    London, Sheed and Ward, 1973.
Schmaus, Michael: *The Church as Sacrament*,
    London, Sheed and Ward, 1975.
Schreiter, Robert J: *Constructing Local Theologies*,
    London, S C M, 1985.
Segundo, Juan Luis S J: *The Liberation of Theology*,
    Dublin, Gill and Macmillan, 1977.
Semmelroth, Otto: *Church and Sacrament*,
    Indiana, Fides, 1965.
Tracy, David: *The Analogical Imagination*,
    London, S C M, 1981.
    Plurality and Ambiguity: Hermeneutics, Religion, Hope,
    San Francisco, Harper and Row, 1987.
Villa-Vicencio, Charles and de Gruchy, John W (eds.) :
    Resistance and Hope,
    South African Essays in Honour of Beyers Naude,
    Michigan, Eerdmans, 1985.
Vischer, Lukas: *A Documentary History of the Faith and Order
    Movement 1927-1963*,
    St Louis, Bethany Press, 1963.
Walzer, Michael: *The Company of Critics*,
    London, Peter Halban, 1989.
Working Party of Irish Council of Churches and Roman Catholic
Church Joint Group on Social Questions:
    Violence in Ireland, A Report to the Churches
    Belfast, Christian Journals, Dublin, Veritas, 1976.

APPENDIX

HOMILIES, STATEMENTS AND ADDRESSES
OF IRISH ROMAN CATHOLIC BISHOPS

Daly, Cahal: Homilies, Statements and Addresses

The Role and Responsibility of the Churches in the Irish Crisis.
Address to Dublin University Historical Society, 1975.

Interview with James Downey, *The Irish Times*, 16 August, 1976.

Northern Ireland: A Shared Responsibility.
Address to Members of Pax Christi, 14 April, 1978.

Letter to a Northern Ireland Protestant.
The Irish Times, June, 1979.

Violence Destroys the Work of Justice.
The Furrow, February, 1980.

The Pope and Northern Ireland.
The Catholic Herald, 4 February, 1980.

Dialogue for Peace.
Address for World Day of Peace, 14 January, 1983.

Homily at Funeral Mass for Judge William Doyle, 18 January, 1983.

War: The Morality, The Reality, The Myth.
Address at Queen's University, Belfast, 2 February, 1984.

Homily, 17 March, 1984.

Homily at Funeral Mass for Mary Travers, 11 April, 1984.

Youth without Guidance.
Address to Youth Committee for Northern Ireland, 18 June, 1984.

Statement, 14 August, 1984. 'Communities Without Consensus.'
Address at Heythrop College, London, 24 November, 1984.

Statement, 9 December, 1984.

Homily at Funeral Mass for Seamus McAvoy, 2 September, 1985.

Homily for Opening of Laity Week, 27 October, 1985.

We Have Passed from Death to Life.
Homily, 10 November, 1985.

Northern Ireland: Risk and Opportunity for the Churches.
Address to the Conference on the Role of the Churches in
British-Irish Relationships. Dublin, 26 November, 1985.

Homily at Funeral Mass for Martin Quinn, 1 February, 1986.

Homily at Funeral Mass for John O'Neill, 18 March, 1986.

Homily at Ecumenical Service for Pentecost, 18 May, 1986.

Homily at Annual Patrician Pilgrimage, 15 June, 1986.

Homily at Funeral Mass for Martin Duffy, 22 July, 1986.

Homily at Funeral Mass for Patrick McAllister, 28 August, 1986.

Homily at Funeral Mass for Raymond Mooney, 19 September,
1986.

Peace Begins With Me.
Homily at Mass for Peace, 5 October, 1986.

Call to Commitment.
Address in St Anne's Cathedral, 16 March, 1987.

Statement Regarding the Funeral of Laurence Marley, 10 April,
1987.

Homily at Funeral Mass for Gary McCartan, 11 May, 1987.

Homily at Funeral Mass for Manuel Wilson and Danny
O'Connor, 28 June, 1987.

Homily at Funeral Mass for Tommy McAuley, 18 November,
1987.

Law and Mercy.
Homily in Belfast, 28 February, 1988.

The Challenge to Christian Conscience.
Statement, 22 March, 1988.

Homily at Funeral Masses for Paul McBride, Damian Devlin,
Stephen McGahan, 18 May, 1988.

Statement at the Murder of Six British Soldiers at Lisburn,
19 June, 1988.

Northern Ireland – Finding a Way Forward.
Address at Corrymeela Conference, 8 October, 1988.

Statement on Recent Murders, 11 April, 1989.

Homily at Funeral Mass for Malachy Trainor, 17 May, 1989.

Homily at Funeral Mass for John Devine, 26 July, 1989.

Homily at Funeral Mass for Patricia McKenna, 5 September, 1989.

Homily at Funeral Mass for James Henry Babington, 6 October,
1989.

Daly, Edward: Homilies, Statements and Addresses

Homily, after Ordination as Bishop, St Eugene's Cathedral, Derry,
1 April, 1974.

Homily, St Mary's, Creggan, 3 April, 1974.

Homily, Castlederg, 5 April, 1974.

Homily, Long Kesh, 5 May, 1974.

Homily at Opening of Holy Year, 2 June, 1974.

Homily at Funeral Mass for Judge Rory Conaghan, 18 September,
1974.

Homily at World Day of Peace, 1 January, 1975.

Statement on I.R.A. Ceasefire, 16 January, 1975.

Address to Clergy at Corrymeela, 30 January, 1975.

Statement on Death of Policeman, 11 May, 1975.

Statement on Death of Policeman, 31 July, 1975.

Pastoral Letter to Priests and People of Derry Diocese, 24 August, 1975.

Address at International Conference, Edinburgh, 6 September, 1975.

Statement on Death of Mr Stott, 25 November, 1975.

Statement on Deaths of Mr Mitchell and Mr McNaul, 2 December, 1975.

Statement on Recent Violence, 15 February, 1976.

Homily at Funeral Mass for Colin Lynch, 20 February, 1976.

Statement on Shooting, 18 May, 1976.

Statement on I.R.A. Threat, 23 September, 1976.

Statement on Murders of Joseph Glover and John Toland, 23 November, 1976.

Homily at Funeral Mass for John Toland, 25 November, 1976.

The Priest and Violence.
Address to Young Priests, 5 January, 1977.

Homily at Funeral Mass for Michael McHugh, 24 January, 1977.

Address to Delegates to International Consultation on Non-Violent Alternatives, 24 April, 1977.

Statement on Visit to Long Kesh, 27 April, 1978.

Statement on Bombing, 20 November, 1978.

Statement on Murder of Patrick Duffy, 27 November, 1978.

Statement on Murder of Christopher Watson, 19 July, 1980.

Statement on Workers' Walkout, 10 November, 1980.

Statement on Murder of Soldier, 13 November, 1980.

Statement on Deaths in Cregan, Derry, 20 April, 1981.

Statement on Death of Bobby Sands, 5 May, 1981.

Statement on Death of Patsy O'Hara, 22 May, 1981.

Statement on Long Kesh Hunger Strike, 30 July,1981.

Statement on Death of Kevin Lynch, 1 August, 1981.

Statement on Murder of Hector Hall, 6 October, 1981.

Statement on Murder of Mr McClintock, 18 November, 1981.

Pastoral Letter to Priests and People of the Derry Diocese, 22 November, 1981.

Letter to Catholic People of the Parishes of Derry City, 4 April, 1982.

Statement on Death of Stephen McConomy, 19 April, 1982.

Statement on Murder of Eamonn Bradley, 28 August, 1982.

Address to St Columb's College Past Pupils, 19 November, 1982.

Statement on Ballykelly Bombing, 7 December, 1982.

Statement on Shooting of Neil McMonagle, 3 February, 1983.

Statement on Murder of Members of Kelly Family, 11 May, 1983.

Statement Regarding Shane Paul O'Doherty, 1 March, 1984.

Homily at Funeral Mass for Michael Devine, 10 September, 1984.

On Being a Bishop.
Address in Heritage Library, Derry, 28 November, 1984.

Statement on Shooting at Gransha Hospital, 7 December, 1984.

Statement on Deaths in Strabane and Derry, 25 February, 1985.

Homily at Mass for Peace in Cork, 3 March, 1985.

Address to St Columb's College Past Pupils, 18 October, 1985.

Homily in St Eugene's Cathedral, 31 August, 1986.

Statement on Squatting, 9 February, 1987.

Statement on Murders in Magee College, 26 March, 1987.

Homily at Funeral Mass for Dermot Hackett, 25 May, 1987.

Statement on Funerals, 30 October, 1987.

Homily at Funeral Mass for Sheila Lewis and Sean Dalton, 3 September, 1988.

Statement on Sion Mills Bombing, 18 January, 1990.

Statement on Murder of Roger Bradley, 7 April, 1990.

Other Statements, Homilies and Addresses from Roman Catholic Bishops and the Hierarchy

Conway, William: *'Statements by Cardinal Conway and Joint Statements on Northern Ireland Situation, 1968-1972.'* Unofficial and Unpublished Collection from The Catholic Press and Information Office, Dublin.

Statement on Violence from the Irish Catholic Bishops' Conference, 13 October, 1976.

Statement on Murders in Comber from the Irish Bishops, 24 February, 1978.

Statement on Hunger Strike by Northern Catholic Bishops, 28 November, 1980.

Statement on Hunger Strike from Irish Catholic Bishops' Conference, 17 June, 1981.

Pastoral Letter from Catholic Bishops of North to Priests and People, 17 January, 1982.

Statement by Northern Catholic Bishops, 4 July, 1983.

Statement from Irish Catholic Bishops, 9 November, 1987.

Statement from Irish Catholic Bishops, 16 March, 1988.